George W. Liebmann is a lawyer and historian specializing in American and international history. His publications include *Diplomacy Between the Wars: Five Diplomats and the Shaping of the Modern World* and *The Last American Diplomat: John D. Negroponte and the Changing Face of US Diplomacy* and *The Fall of the House of Speyer* (all I.B.Tauris)

"Liebmann's expertise in American government and its history is evident throughout. He makes the historical development of institutions come alive by putting faces and personalities on those who promoted them. Readers can discover how newspaper magnate Joseph Pulitzer was instrumental in the home rule movement and why so many state universities have a 'Morrill Hall' on their campuses. Liebmann's look back at these entrepreneurs of the public sector enriches our understanding of our system and, one hopes, will inspire others to try more innovative solutions to ongoing problems."

William A. Fischel,
Professor of Economics and Hardy Professor of
Legal Studies, Dartmouth College

"How refreshing to read a book about political science from the bottom up, about political ideas that actually work, and about the innovators who came up with successful practical schemes that have empowered American citizens and communities over the years. Anyone who feels resigned to over-regulation and hyper-centralization will find a bracing antidote in George Liebmann's own proposals for workable improvements to our systems of taxation, education, and urban renewal."

Mary Ann Glendon,
Learned Hand Professor of Law,
Harvard University and author of *The Forum and the Tower:
How Scholars and Politicians have Imagined the World from Plato
to Eleanor Roosevelt*

Also by George W. Liebmann

The Fall of the House of Speyer: The Story of a Banking Dynasty (2015)

The Last American Diplomat: John D. Negroponte and the Changing Face of US Diplomacy (2012)

Diplomacy Between the Wars: Five Diplomats and the Shaping of the Modern World (2007)

The Common Law Tradition: A Collective Portrait of Five Legal Scholars (2004)

Six Lost Leaders: Prophets of Civil Society (2002)

Solving Problems Without Large Government: Devolution, Fairness and Equality (2000), reprinted as *Neighborhood Futures* (2002)

The Gallows in the Grove: Civil Society in American Law (1997)

The Little Platoons: Sub-Local Governments in Modern History (1995)

AMERICA'S POLITICAL
INVENTORS
The Lost Art of Legislation

GEORGE W. LIEBMANN

I.B. TAURIS
LONDON · NEW YORK

Published in 2018 by
I.B.Tauris & Co. Ltd
London • New York
www.ibtauris.com

International Library of Historical Studies 112

ISBN: 978 1 78831 124 3
eISBN: 978 1 78672 301 7
ePDF: 978 1 78673 301 6

A full CIP record for this book is available from the British Library
A full CIP record is available from the Library of Congress

Library of Congress Catalog Card Number: available

Printed and bound by TJ International Ltd, Padstow PL28 8RW

MIX
Paper from
responsible sources
FSC® C013056
FSC
www.fsc.org

CONTENTS

LIST OF ILLUSTRATIONS

INTRODUCTION

"Social engineering," a practice decried by the American Right, has a bad name. But at its best, it involves the declaration of "Uniform rules laid down in advance"— Friedrich Hayek's definition of the Rule of Law. Such rules enable and empower those to whom they are addressed, leaving them free to grasp opportunities and organize their own lives within broadly defined parameters—to enjoy "leave to live by no man's leave / Underneath the law."

There has been little such lawmaking of late.

Thirty years have passed since any domestic legislation of major import to citizens generally has been enacted by Congress. The Johnson and Nixon Administrations sponsored the Civil Rights Acts of 1964 and 1965, Medicare, air and water pollution control, and the higher education loan program. Since then, Congress's domestic output has been trivial—pretentiously trivial, voluminously trivial, but trivial. This is even true of the voluminous and much-touted "Obamacare" legislation, which essentially refines and enlarges existing law relating to assigned risk insurance exchanges. The same is true of the output of state legislatures since the enactment of the Uniform Commercial Code in the 1960s. There have been tax bills that sometimes have included major alterations in rates, but no innovations in principle. There has been a steady and thoughtless accretion to federal criminal jurisdiction in omnibus bills that are hundreds of pages long and include dozens of new capital offenses.[1] There has been the war on drugs, with its unparalleled assertion of jurisdiction over possession of small quantities of even mild drugs—an assertion that the Supreme Court, in the *Oakland Cannabis* case,[2] said raised constitutional problems, only to back away from this suggestion in the later *Gonzales v. Raich* case.[3] The airline, transportation, banking, public utility, and communications industries have been deregulated, generally pursuant to vague mandates addressed to administrative agencies; this has produced some benefits, but also the savings and loan, sub-prime mortgage, and Enron scandals. Finally, we have the Bush education law, which proceeded, like much federal legislation, by directing vague mandates to state and local governments that benefit from modest amounts of federal aid.

A statute, Learned Hand once said, should proliferate a purpose.[4] Its meaning should be understood by the citizenry. Its values should be shared by the people, inhabitants of a commercial republic with a tradition of limited government. It should not depend much on the competence and discretion of administrators, for America has never really had a professional civil service and the legislature's delegates cannot be relied upon to be either competent or discreet. If it is federal legislation, it should be executed by federal officers; the framers of the Constitution did not intend for the federal government to rule by coercing the states; this was one of the vices of the Articles of Confederation.

We live in a period in which:

> few laws were designed for more than a tiny minority to comprehend. In the nineteenth century, democracy measured public policy against a universalist standard, an ideal of one land policy or one corporate policy for all. Separate laws for separate groups automatically suggested corruption. The model for the twentieth century was the diametric opposite.[5]

The broad delegations of power to executive agencies were described by Theodore Lowi in *The End of Liberalism*: "Interest-group liberalism seeks pluralistic government, in which there is no formal specification of means or of ends. In a pluralistic government there is, therefore, no substance. Neither is there procedure. There is only process."[6] The result is a working Constitution described by Lowi as follows:

[The President] is authorized to use any powers, real or imagined, to set our nation to rights by making any rules or regulations the President deems appropriate; the President may subdelegate this authority to any other official or agency [...] actual policymaking will come from a process of tripartite bargaining between the specialized administrators, relevant members of Congress, and the representatives of self-selected organized interests.[7]

We here recall some laws of the earlier type. Their stories and those of the remarkable men who were their framers are interesting in their own right, and like parables or fables supply instruction that is much needed. After these verses have been read, we may consider how to apply these lessons.

1

John Locke and Southern Plantations

The character of today's Southern local government owes something to its colonial heritage. Although several American constitutions carried with them the influence of great political theorists, including Jefferson, Madison and James Wilson, few realize that Southern government, at its inception, also owes something to one of the greatest of political theorists, John Locke. Locke's *Fundamental Constitutions of Carolina* (1669) will not be found in most collections of his works, though the manuscript is written in his own hand; he was 37 years old and secretary to Sir Anthony Ashley Cooper, third Earl of Shaftesbury,[1] and many later writers prefer to assume that its text is not chargeable to him.[2] Both Locke's career and some of the Lockean themes in the *Fundamental Constitutions* make this conclusion questionable. Moreover, a letter from Sir Peter Colleton to Locke written in October 1673 refers to "that excellent forme of government in the composure of which you had so great a hand."[3] Daniel Defoe, in his remonstrance on behalf of the Carolina dissenters, published in 1705 as "Party-Tyranny," referred to:

> those Constitutions I know have obtained upon the World to be the contrivance of the Old Earl of S[haftes]bury; but I think I have very good authority to assure the World Mr. Lock[e] had the Right of Parentage to the former [...] [T]hey hustled the Infant Government

1. John Locke, 1632–1704 (Library of Congress)

into the World without Leading-strings, and turned it loose before it could stand alone.[4]

Letters to Locke by Nicolas Toinard and Henri Justel refer to "vos constitutions" and "vos loix," and it has been shown that Locke was involved with the affairs of Carolina almost constantly from 1668 until his death in 1704.[5] By 1763, Voltaire had declared: "behold Carolina, of which the wise Locke was the legislator."[6]

In 1720, *A Collection of Several Pieces of Mr. John Locke* was published in London with the Constitution of Carolina the first.[7] The prefatory letter by a Mr. (Pierre) Des Meizeaux related:

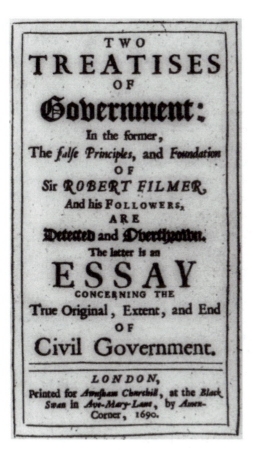

TWO
TREATISES
OF
𝔊𝔬𝔳𝔢𝔯𝔫𝔪𝔢𝔫𝔱:
In the former,
The *falſe Principles*, and *Foundation*
OF
Sir *ROBERT FILMER*,
And his FOLLOWERS,
ARE
𝔇𝔢𝔱𝔢𝔠𝔱𝔢𝔡 and 𝔒𝔳𝔢𝔯𝔱𝔥𝔯𝔬𝔴𝔫.
The latter is an
ESSAY
CONCERNING THE
True Original, Extent, and End
OF
Civil Government.

LONDON,
Printed for *Awnſham Churchill*, at the *Black*
Swan in *Ave-Mary-Lane*, by *Amen-*
Corner, 1690.

2. Title page of John Locke, *Two Treatises of Government* (London,
1690) (Library of Congress)

You have here the Constitution printed from Mr. Locke's copy,
wherein are several amendments made with his own hand. He had
presented it as a work of his to one of his friends, who was pleased to
communicate it to me.

Des Meizeaux, a Huguenot refugee from the Edict of Nantes, was
an associate of Locke's patron Lord Shaftesbury. The first edition
was published only 16 years after Locke's death in 1704.

It is a distinct understatement for one writer to say that Locke was "the author with his master in a way not yet fully worked out of the notorious Constitutions of Carolina."[8] For, according to Neal Wood,

> Locke was involved in the scheme as Secretary of the Lords Proprietary in 1668–75 and he later performed the same function for the Council for Trade and Plantations under Shaftesbury's presidency. Most important, from 1696 to 1700 Locke was a commissioner of the Board of Trade, an advisory and policy-making body that became the architect of England's mercantile imperialism. In all these positions he participated in the framing of domestic as well as colonial agrarian policy.[9]

Locke's biographer Maurice Cranston observes:

> Minutes in Locke's hand show that he attended regularly in his capacity as secretary the meetings of the Lords Proprietors of Carolina until June 1675. The Lords Proprietors, who had powers to grant titles of nobility, bestowed on him in April 1671 the rank of landgrave in the aristocracy of Carolina—the title to be his and his heirs' forever. At the same time they gave him four thousand "barona" or estates of land in the colony. As the aristocracy of Carolina never materialized, the title was an insubstantial one and even the land appears to have yielded no rent.[10]

It is said that this was "contrary to the King's Charter which stated that only inhabitants and not individuals living in England could be given such status."[11] The declaration of the proprietors of April 4, 1671, declaring him landgrave by its terms, was given because of "his great prudence, learning and industry, both in settling the form of government and in planning colonies on the Ashley River."[12]

Cranston cites a "notebook Locke kept in 1672 [which] contains a great number of entries on the subject of Carolina."[13] As noted by Barbara Arneil, "Cranston destroys the attempts of Victorian biographers to make Locke a political innocent in all of Shaftesbury's intrigues."[14] Locke became a merchant adventurer, investing £200 in an enterprise in the Bahamas (which had been ceded to the Lords Proprietors of Carolina in 1670) and sold his stock at a profit;[15] he also invested £600 in the Royal African Company in 1674–5.[16] He was said by Cranston (and later by Mary Ann Glendon) to consider that "a life of action was a necessary part of the life of reason [...] a man could not discover truth by sitting still and thinking but only by personal experience of life."[17] Although the *Fundamental Constitutions* may be "the ugly duckling of Lockean scholarship," his responsibility for and annotations on them have been noted by a number of scholars; the only provision from which he explicitly noted his dissent was Article XCVI of the first printed version declaring the Anglican church to be the official religion.[18]

Both Locke and Shaftesbury believed in the economic benefits of religious toleration. Both spent time in Holland, which epitomized the commercial benefits of toleration. Shaftesbury was said to be "the complete progressive capitalist in politics; he might almost have been invented by Marx."[19] The *Fundamental Constitutions* reflected "interest in moving the rich—that is, those who had money and the ability to plant— to the new world in order to ensure the success of the plantation."[20] The land grants and aristocratic titles were thus not as much at variance with Locke's conception of natural rights in property subdued by labor as might be supposed. Locke was hostile to free appropriation of frontier lands, deploring the failure of Virginia to settle colonists in towns.[21] "Labour, rather than occupation, would begin property. And those who tilled, enclosed, and cultivated the soil would be its owners. England superseded the right of occupation by the Amerindians by virtue of their specific form of labour."[22] He was an opponent of idleness and beggary as they produced "relaxation of discipline and the corruption of manners, virtue and industry."[23] His views on beggary and idleness closely resembled those giving rise to the laws of settlement and to the Poor Law Amendment Act of 1835.

Locke, however,

> adhered to an ontological distinction drawn between the Amerindian
> as "natural" pre-Christian man who, with the fullness of time would
> be transformed from his natural state into civil Christian man, and
> the African black who was somehow less than human. In other
> words, the latter could be enslaved while the former could not.[24]

He was never explicit about this. His "just war" theory, which
upheld the temporary enslavement of Native Americans, could not
extend to African-Americans, whose slavery was hereditary and
extended to their families and was not founded on conquest.[25] This
lacuna did not go unnoticed: "how is it that we hear the loudest
yelps for liberty among the drivers of negroes?", Samuel Johnson
asked,[26] while Jeremy Bentham summarized Locke's thought as:
"Property the only object of care to government. Persons possess-
ing it alone to be represented. West Indies the meridian for these
principles of the liberty-champion."[27] Jeremy Waldron refers to
the problem as "a contradiction which exists only by virtue of our
own late twentieth or early twenty-first century ideas about the
political integrity of an intellectual life."[28]

The proprietors' charter gave them wide powers, with three
restrictions. They were required to recognize the "liberties, franchises and privileges of Englishmen," to uphold freedom of conscience, and to subject taxes to the "approbation of freemen."[29] It
also declared: "You are to order the people to plant towns."[30]

The *Constitutions* did not assail but reinforced the institution of
slavery, with its later resonance. Article CX referred to a freeman's
"absolute power over his negro slaves." The reference to "power" was
added in Locke's own hand; there is no "mistaking either his tacit
commitment to this brutal provision or to the hold the master-slave
relationship had over his political imagination."[31] This was to be
unaffected by religious principles, a paradoxical outcome of Locke's
belief in religious toleration. Article CVII provided: "Religion
ought to alter nothing in any man's civil state or right." Articles
CVII and XCVII recognized the right of slaves to choose their religion without the threat of expulsion or ill-treatment but without

affecting "that civil dominion his master has over him." One was
a freeman according to Article XCV if one acknowledged "a God
and that God is publicly and solemnly worshipped." "Any seven or
more persons, agreeing in any religion, shall constitute a church or
profession," so that "Jews, heathens and other dissenters from the
purity of Christian religion may not be scared and kept at a distance
from it" (Art. XCVII). "No person of any other church or profession shall disturb or molest any religious assembly" (Art. CII).
"No person whatsoever shall disturb, molest or persecute another
for his speculative opinions in religion, or his way of worship" (Art.
CIX). Provision was made for affirmations as well as oaths (Art.
C). Naturalization required only subscription to the *Fundamental
Constitutions* (Art. CXVIII). It is alleged that the single provision
added by Shaftesbury was the provision for establishment of the
Anglican church in Article XCVI. In planning the future of the
colony, Article XLII preferred "numbers of men [...] to largeness
of dominions." The purpose of the government, per the preamble,
was that it be "made most agreeable to the monarchy, under which
we live, and of which this province is part." The preamble therefore
denies the right of revolution. Slavery was unconvincingly legiti-
mized on the basis of slaves' status as "captives taken in a just war"
(Art. LXXXV), in which "by his fault [he] forfeited his life, by some
act that deserves death" (Art. XXIII). Slavery is "the state of war
continued, between a lawful conqueror and a captive."

The *Constitutions* resembled New England town constitutions
in being a covenant requiring freemen to accept its contents in
writing before the registrar of a precinct (Art. CXVII), including a commitment to maintain the established form of government. There is a restriction on the right of emigration in Article
CXXI that appears to qualify Locke's compact or consent theory,[32]
though its last clause is ambiguous:

> He, that has once, by actual agreement [...] given his consent to be
> of any commonweal, is perpetually and indispensably obliged to be
> and remain unalterably a subject to it [...] unless by any calamity,
> the government, he was under, comes to be dissolved; or else by
> some public act cuts him off from being any longer a member of it.

The right of suffrage for Locke attached only to those who bore the burdens of taxation, as stated in the *Treatise on Government*. Article IV assigns one-fifth of the land to the Lords Proprietors, another fifth to the lesser nobility, and the balance to the freeholders. Each county contains four precincts inhabited by freeholders and eight baronies. Candidates must have 500 acres and electors 50 acres. The preamble disclaims any purpose to "erect a numerous democracy."

Each county was to consist of eight seignories, eight baronies, and four precincts; each precinct was to consist of six colonies. Each seignory, barony, and colony was to consist of 12,000 acres. Thus each county was to have 480,000 acres, or 750 square miles (Arts. III and IV). Each county was to have a landgrave with four baronies and two cassiques with two baronies; these collectively were to be the hereditary nobility (Art. IX). Each barony had a manorial court; non-residents had rights of appeal. The *Constitution* provided for serfs or leet-men who became such by entering themselves as such in the court registry; leet-men had no appeal from the manorial courts and could not leave the manor without written permission; their descendants had similar status (Arts. XXII–XXV). On marriage, they were entitled to ten acres of land and were to accord the manorial lord not more than one-eighth of the crops (Art. XXVI). They were the equivalent of English copy-holders. Elections were to be by ballot, a progressive provision for the time (Art. XXXII). There were elaborate provisions for courts, councils, and numerous other public offices (Art. LXIII). One of the courts was accorded "the license of printing" (Art. XXXV). Article LXIV unequivocally prohibited double jeopardy. A high steward's court was authorized to lay out towns and construct buildings; persons whose land was taken had the right to compensation for damages (Art. XLIV). Lawyers were frowned upon; "It shall be a base and vile thing to plead for money or reward" (Art. LXX). Legal academics were also frowned on: "all manner of comments and expositions on […] law, are absolutely prohibited," since these "have great inconveniences, and serve only to obscure and perplex." The object was "to keep the judiciary from falling into the hands of lawyers who might usurp the prerogatives of the nobility, a legal system simple enough to be administered by aristocrats untrained in the law"[33] (Art. LXXX).

There were to be majority verdicts of 12 jurors (Art. LXIX). There was a tricameral parliament; any proprietor could require acts to be voted on separately by proprietors, landgraves, cassiques, and precinct representatives, all of whom had to approve the acts (Art. LXXVII). There was a 100-year sunset provision for all statutes "to avoid multiplicity of laws" (Art. LXXIX). All marriages had to be civilly registered to be valid (Art. LXXXVII). Incorporated towns were to have a mayor and council chosen by householders (Art. LXXXII).

There was a provision for military service of those aged between 16 and 60 in Article CXVI. The 1682 version in Article CXXI expanded on this by providing that the resulting militia shall be mustered and exercised,

> and there must never be in Carolina a select militia, wherein one part of the people shall be armed and the other not, nor any standing forces in pay, except only in such frontier garrisons, with such number of Soldiers in them, as the palatine's court, with the Consent of the grand council and parliament shall appoint.

As Murrin points out:

> In England, part of the transition from medieval to modern was the crown's assault on bastard feudalism, which meant disarming most of the population in the interests of public order. The colonies moved in the opposite direction, compelling all freemen to arm.[34]

The 1682 changes also allowed grand juries to make proposals to the Carolina parliament, proposed secret balloting in the Grand Council, provided that proprietors' deputies would not lose their posts for misdemeanors, provided for the drawing of juries by lot, and added provisions for amendment.[35]

Very detailed provisions about inheritance and conveyance of land were designed to freeze the existing social order: "For it is as bad as a state of war for men that are in want to have the making

of laws over men that have estates."[36] The 1682 version of the
Fundamental Constitutions had appended to it elaborate rules of
precedency, with authority in a Chamberlain's Court to define yet
more rules:[37]

Rules of Precedency
I
The Lords Proprietors, the eldest in age first and so in order
II
The eldest sons of the Lords Proprietors, the eldest in age first and
    so in order
III
The landgraves of the Grand Council, he that hath been longest of
    the Grand Council first, and so in order
IV
The caciques of the Grand Council, he that hath been longest of the
    Grand Council first, and so in order.

And so on.

The provisions for indivisible hereditary manors had mixed
appeal to settlers who were mostly younger sons victimized by
primogeniture in England and Barbados.[38] Central to the design
was:

religious toleration, a popular instead of a standing army, and the
use of the ballot rather than the "lot." At the heart of the document was the concept that power follows property, a concept which
had received its most cogent expression in Harrington's *Oceana*: "to
maintain social balance and avoid a numerous democracy."[39]

The peculiar titles of nobility were due to "a requirement of the
Palatinate grant which permits the proprietors to create social tiers
but not to replicate titles already in use in England." The grants
were to be indivisible, to ensure that the proportions of classes
remained constant.[40]

Cooper was one of several proprietors who had gained title to
all the land between Virginia and South Carolina by royal charter
in 1663. He was credited by some with "liberality and tolerance

in religious things and philosophic idealism," while being charged by others with being "violent in his passions, implacable in his malice, without principle, honor or conscience."[41] The effort to relaunch a failed colony presupposed a more active role for the proprietors in its development. Galenson points out that:

> The constitution provided for a class of wealthy aristocrats, who were to make large investments in the colony and receive great estates, a large class of lesser property-owners who would pay quit-rents to the colony's proprietors, and another class of tenants who would have no political role. The constitution also recognized that blacks would be held as chattel slaves. Political stability was to be gained in the colony by giving the primary political and judiciary positions to the nobility, while creating a limited degree of democracy by allowing all landowners to vote for representatives to a parliament that could accept or reject legislation initiated by a council of the noblemen.[42]

The three-level government based on proprietors, council, and assembly has been characterized as "proprietary feudalism": "one aspect of the Harringtonian idealism that the proprietors tried to inflict on unwilling settlers."[43] "Access to fresh lands, for example, undercut primogeniture, entail, and the whole social logic that stressed transmission to the next generation of a consolidated paternal estate."[44] "The settlement initiated by Ashley's efforts centered around the town that would later be named Charleston grew into the prosperous colony of South Carolina."[45]

"The greater economic power conferred on settlers by the New World's labor scarcity prevented these English tenures and practices from taking hold."[46] Efforts were made to secure formal ratification of the *Fundamental Constitutions* as late as 1705. Half-a-century after their first promulgation, the planters, who were operating a plantation economy based on slave labor, formed their own government and withdrew recognition from the proprietors. In 1720, at the request of the new government, South Carolina became a royal colony. The proprietors retained their lands until 1729, when they surrendered their land rights in exchange for payments from the English exchequer.[47]

In spite of their seemingly reactionary provisions for titles of nobility, or more accurately because of them, the *Constitutions* were an effective recruiting device. Charleston and its surrounding area attracted immigrants from Barbados, the provisions legitimating African-American slavery doubtless being helpful in this respect. The provisions relating to religious tolerance, more advanced than those of any other colony save Rhode Island, attracted Jews, French Huguenots, and other religious dissenters; the Jewish community of Charleston was the most prominent such community in the South. Among those acquiring 1,000-acre tracts between 1670 and 1720, 33 were from Barbados, 35 were from England, and 30 were French Huguenots.[48] In the earlier period between 1660 and 1670, 13 were Barbadians and eight were from England. By 1692, six of the 20 members of the lower house were Huguenots; they represented about 4 percent of the population. There were 500 Huguenots by 1700.[49]

As Hagy points out, "For a generation after the Revolution, more Jews resided in Charleston than in any other city in North America. There they gained full economic and political rights much earlier than elsewhere in the western world."[50] There were roughly 3,000 Jews in Charleston before the Civil War; as early as 1692 five or six of the leading merchants were drawn from their number.[51] Following the revocation of the Edict of Nantes by Louis XIV of France in 1685, there was substantial immigration by French Huguenots. Initiation of laws by a 50-member Grand Council, modeled after that of the Venetian Republic, was abandoned in 1691, its principle being that "laws should be initiated by the best and resolved by the most." In 1694, unanimous jury verdicts replaced those based on majority vote.[52] In 1697, citizenship was expressly given to all immigrants and freedom of conscience was guaranteed to all save Catholics. In 1704, religious tests for voting were eliminated. Thereafter a reaction set in; the franchise was limited to Christians in 1716 and to Protestants in 1759. Later legislation restored the franchise to Jews, but barred them from office; all religious qualifications for office and franchise were finally eliminated in 1770.[53]

Charleston thus became the most cosmopolitan of Southern cities. Some form of tolerance was a characteristic attribute of the proprietary, as distinct from royal, colonies: "the concession by all promoters of colonization of liberty of conscience to those who believed in God as an indispensable privilege offered to attract settlers."[54] As suggested by Craven:

> When its early history is properly viewed, the cardinal fact becomes [...] the successful administration of a shrewdly conceived land policy. Feudal terminology and feudal concepts of social and political organization notwithstanding, the hard reality underlying the proprietors' land policy was the now tried and true headright system. This it was that brought increasing numbers from Barbados, Bermuda, England, New York, Ireland and France each to pick for himself a part of the land and by the simple process established to secure a title to it, to clear the land and then to plant it.[55]

In 1692 the system was supplemented by giving new migrants "headright" grants of land of 50 acres, an anticipation of the later western homestead laws.[56] "Except in New England, the 'headright' system was the usual route to land ownership in colonial America. It was designed to encourage men of means to settle workingmen on the land."[57] The proposed manorial courts were stillborn. Leet-men disappeared from the 1682 and 1698 draft constitutions; the shortage of labor in America and the availability of land on the frontier precluded creation of a permanently indentured class of serfs. There were only 210 white servants by 1703 and 120 by 1708. In 1703 there were 4,220 whites, 3,250 blacks, and 800 Native American slaves; creation of the last group appears contrary to Locke's intent, though it was rationalized on the basis that the Native Americans were captives in just wars: "idolatry ignorance or mistake gives us no right to expel or use [the natives] ill."[58] The settlers fomented wars among the Native Americans; the Native American slave population ultimately disappeared. In 1696 a harsh slave law drawn from that of Barbados was enacted, requiring written permission to leave, mandating search of slave quarters for weapons, and providing harsh punishments, including branding and castration, for runaways.[59] Bacon's Rebellion in Virginia, a revolt of the "leet-men," resulted in the replacement of white servants with black slaves. Later, in a report to the British

Board of Trade, Locke was to lament: "the great men of the country have 20, 25, or 30 thousand acres of land in their hands and there is hardly any left for the poor people to take upp."[60]

A drastically simplified version of the *Fundamental Constitutions*, reduced to 41 articles, was proposed in 1698.[61] The *Constitutions* applied only in an attenuated way to the Albemarle settlement in North Carolina, where the economy was not based on slave labor gangs harvesting rice and indigo. Aside from two landgraves, there was no institutionalized aristocracy in North Carolina. By 1691, it had 4,000 settlers and was effectively independent of its proprietors, though they did not formally surrender their charter over Albemarle until 1729. It was later said of North Carolina that "the North Carolina continuity is of people, not of buildings, of the pioneer possibility of equality and comradeship in equality."[62]

The aristocratic elements in the *Constitutions* ultimately disappeared in South Carolina as well as North Carolina: "the utopian elements [derived from Harrington's *Oceana*] quickly disintegrated," but in South Carolina they left a residue:

> Pure deference in which the many willingly yield to the superior judgment of the few probably does characterize some of these regimes. South Carolina by mid [eighteenth] century had few contested elections and not many voters were likely to show up.[63]

According to Murrin, "The planter elites of South Carolina and Virginia were decidedly oligarchic. They offered scant opportunity for a small planter to cross the watershed that separated ordinary mortals from gentlemen,"[64] although a freeman who acquired 3,000 acres could have his estate declared to be a manor.[65] He further points out that:

> Slave-produced rice and indigo brought great wealth to South Carolina. Indeed, the extreme wealth of the planters and merchants of Charleston was not found anywhere else in the continental colonies. Moreover the number of slaves per individual owner in the Charleston district was larger than elsewhere in the mainland colonies.[66]

According to Middleton and Lombard, "By the middle of the eighteenth century, a local aristocracy had emerged though it owed nothing to the proprietors and placed little reliance on a yeomanry."[67] By 1774, per capita wealth in Charleston was £2,300, four times that in the Chesapeake, six times that in Philadelphia and New York. There were 12,000 colonists by 1775, 92 percent of them slaveholders, with 43 slaves per head. "The allure of Charles Town was so great and the white population of the countryside so small that in South Carolina there were no county courts or county based politics and little county society."[68] The planters were "just as reluctant as the executive party to de-centralize governmental authority within the State."[69] Even the 1895 Constitution provided for no locally elected governmental bodies.[70] As Hawke points out: "[G]overnment and society, stripped of their strange names, and the landed aristocracy, minus its hereditary nobility, bore a striking resemblance in the 18th century to that envisioned by Locke and Shaftesbury in the 17th."[71] The number of slaves increased from 1,500 in 1690 to 2,400 in 1700, 4,300 in 1710, 12,000 in 1720, 20,000 in 1730, 39,200 in 1740 and 57,000 in 1760.[72] The death rates were such that only continuing imports gave rise to an increase in the slave population.

"The men who went to Virginia and the Carolinas," James Bryce wrote,

were not Puritans nor did they mostly go in families or groups of families from the same neighbourhood. Many were casual adventurers, often belonging to the upper class, with no such experience of, or attachment to, local self-government as the men of Massachusetts or Connecticut. They settled in a region […] where there was little need of concentration for the purposes of defense […] Population was thinly scattered; estates were large; the soil was fertile and soon enriched its owners. Thus a semi-feudal society grew up, in which authority naturally fell to the landowners […] [W]hen local divisions had to be created, these were made large enough to include a considerable area of territory and number of landowning gentlemen. They were therefore rural divisions, counties framed on the model of English counties.[73]

In fact, however, the real unit of local government in early South Carolina was the ecclesiastical parish, which allowed dissenters as well as Anglicans to vote and which became responsible for poor relief and even the conduct of state elections.[74]

Locke's *Constitutions* cast a long shadow:

> In the first place, the *Constitutions* provided for a policy of religious toleration in Carolina that profoundly affected the colony's history for half a century by attracting many religious dissenters to it. In the second place, the land system proposed in the *Constitutions* had far-reaching effects. Ashley hoped to foster a landed aristocracy in the colony and by the middle of the eighteenth century a landed gentry had emerged [...] no one can deny that the *Constitutions* with its provisions for a local aristocracy and incredibly large land grants speeded the development of a landed gentry in South Carolina [...] [The slavery provision was] of crucial importance in shaping the development of Carolina.[75]

There were also cultural effects. The gentry's major interest was estate management at the expense of education, which it was feared would disturb the social order; a jaundiced critic in 1725 said that they devoted themselves to "eating, drinking, lolling, smoking, and sleeping" and were "to the last degree ignorant and opinionated."[76] "Living in idle ease," De Tocqueville said,

> he has the tastes of idle men [...] he passionately loves hunting and war, he pleases himself with the most violent exercises of the body, the use of arms is familiar to him, and from his childhood he has learned to stake his life in single combat [...] [T]oday, it is only the North that has ships, manufacturers, railroads, and canals [...] [T]he younger ones, without having the same wealth as the eldest, remain an idle caste. What would the poor man of Europe do if, coming to seek comfort and happiness in the New World, he went to inhabit a country where work is tainted with ignominy?[77]

Tocqueville also forecast that:

> the abolition of slavery in the South will increase the repugnance for blacks felt by the white population. [...] [T]he legislation of

the Southern states relative to slaves in our day presents a sort of unheard-of atrocity [...] They have violated all the rights of humanity toward the black, and then they have instructed him in the worth and inviolability of these rights. [...] If one refuses freedom to Negroes in the South they will in the end seize it violently themselves; if one grants it to them, they will not be slow to abuse it.[78]

By the time Tocqueville wrote, South Carolina and Maryland were the only states to retain substantial property qualifications for voting: 50 acres in each case. In 1790, South Carolina's legislators were the only members of an American assembly who were not paid; "they could defy the proprietors, or later the royal governor, without immediate threat of financial loss." A Representative had to have 500 acres and ten slaves or £500; a Senator twice as much. Voters had to have 50 acres or a town lot or had to pay three shillings in taxes. Representation was allocated according to wealth rather than population, giving the advantage to the low country.[79] There were no colleges in South Carolina until after the American Revolution. Those desiring education were sent to England and indoctrinated in a class system; after 1760 there were three times as many South Carolinians as Virginians at Oxbridge, and more of them at the Inns of Court than those from all the other Southern colonies combined.[80] "[M]asters of slaves feared their education. Rich families hired tutors, but 'poor whites', lacking resources, simply remained illiterate."[81] This "sustained an arrogant and powerful ruling class in the 'colony of a colony' that became South Carolina—one that has been especially virulent as a source of racism throughout its existence."[82] South Carolina was the last state to allow popular election of presidential electors. All this bore fruit at the unanimous 1860 secession convention. The North Carolina and Virginia conventions initially rejected secession; even in Mississippi the vote was close.

Yet Locke and Shaftesbury were successful in what they sought to achieve. Although Dickens was to deride the South Carolinians as "the miserable aristocracy of a false republic," it remains true that "the closest ante-bellum approximation of an upper class was the interwoven cluster of planter families at the head of South Carolina's society and government."[83] One need not advocate a new feudalism to understand that Locke and Shaftesbury had laid hold of an element of human nature underappreciated in the United States: the importance of non-economic incentives. These:

> gave South Carolina's social and political order a very English fla-
> vour […] a large tract of land in the New World along with the Old
> World privileges presumed to go with it […] freedom of worship,
> a powerful advertising tool with which to attract new settlers not
> immediately attracted to land-ownership; a traditional, land-based
> aristocratic perspective […] large-scale planters and successful mer-
> chants held the top, artisans and craftsmen were in the middle, and
> transient or indentured servants and enslaved African Americans
> were at the bottom.[84]

A nation with the egalitarian traditions of the United States is uncomfortable with the conscious creation of elites, even mer-itocratic ones. Yet there are elements of the British honors system that are attractive, and in a troubled time—the late 1930s—Peter Drucker reminded us of the psychological appeal of non-economic incentives in his *End of Economic Man*.[85] So did Simone Weil, in a different way, in her *The Need for Roots*.[86] The multiplication of grass-roots, self-governing institutions is one way of providing such incentives. Greater recognition of excellent performance in high schools is another. Equality, in the sense of a reasonably equal starting line, need not mean mediocrity, though increasingly in America that is its consequence.

2

John Winthrop and the New England Town

The saga of John Winthrop, the great Puritan founder of the Massachusetts Bay Colony, has been said by Oscar Handlin to display a "long conflict between the demands of authority and the permissiveness of freedom."[1] He reacted against the state of English society:

> Why meet we so many wandering ghosts in shape of men, so many spectacles of misery in all our streets, our houses full of victuals and our entries of hunger-starved Christians; our shops full of rich wares and under our stalls lie our own flesh in nakedness. Our people perish for want of sustenance and employment; many others live miserably and not to the honor of so bountiful a housekeeper as the lord of heaven and earth […] [A]ll of our towns complain of the burden of poor people and strive by all means to rid any such as they have and to keep off such as would come to them.[2]

In a "Statement of Common Grievances" written with others in the winter of 1623–4, he protested against the removal of indictments from the localities in which they were found. In the statement he also sought a law to require the planting of two trees for each one felled, another law requiring that lawsuits be finally adjudicated before four court terms had passed, and a law limiting the number of attorneys in each county.[3] In 1628 Winthrop presented a bill to prevent drunkenness by limiting to two-and-a-half

IN HONOR OF THE BIRTHDAY OF GOVERNOR JOHN WINTHROP, BORN JUNE 12, 1587.

3. Gov. John Winthrop. In honor of the birthday of Governor John Winthrop, born June 12, 1587 / K. H. Burn del. (Library of Congress)

barrels the permitted quantity of malt per hogshead of ale. In the same year he also prepared a draft of an assessment bill under which officials were to assess each person's property in light of his trade, occupation, and family responsibilities.[4]

On August 29, 1629, 12 persons signed the "Cambridge Declaration" mutually promising to be ready to sail by March 1 the following year.[5] Winthrop recognized that it was "manifestly dangerous to allow every man to build his own utopia." Winthrop's purpose, in Edmund Morgan's words, was "to leave England altogether yet leave it with the approbation of the King and without repudiating its churches and the Christians in them."[6] Hence a Humble Request for prayers from English churches for the success of the voyage was addressed to them on April 7, 1630.[7] His regime was both authoritarian and communitarian; in forging a durable community he "found answers to some problems that we would rather forget." According to Morison: "Their object was

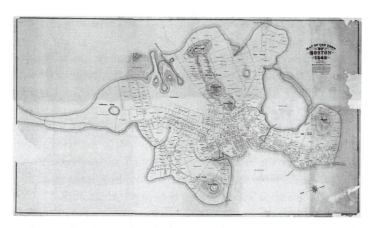

4. Map of the Town of Boston 1648; drawn by Samuel C. Clough, in accordance with information compiled from the records of the colony (from the Samuel Chester Clough research materials toward a topographical history of Boston, www.masshist.org)

not to establish prosperity or prohibition, liberty or democracy, or indeed anything of currently recognized value."[8] As described by the American historian Page Smith:

> Humility, unworldliness, Christian equality—these were the ingredients of small-town "democracy". It provided no room for tolerance of other creeds, religious or political; it was not based on the assumption that government represented a consensus among disparate groups with different interests and different conceptions of the truth. For the town, there was only one truth—its own.[9]

As Morison points out: "We will not often find breadth of mind among the English puritans, but we will find a spiritual depth that belongs only to the great ages of religious experience."[10] Winthrop's doctrine at its inception was a "doctrine of aristocratic stewardship," in the words of the progressive historian Vernon Parrington.[11] But his ideal of the covenanted community resonated in New England and in the places in the Midwest to which New Englanders migrated, and his successive concessions to democracy resulted in the establishment of durable and vital town governments.

Winthrop's first and best-known political discourse was his *Model of Christian Charity*, written in 1630 just prior to or during his voyage to America. In it he expressed hope for a society in which "the rich and mighty should not eat up the poor; nor the poor and despised rise up against their superiors and shake off their yoke." This presupposed a class society on the English model: "under the first are comprehended all such as are able to live comfortably by their own means duly improved, and all others are poor according to the former distribution." "No man is made more honourable or rich out of respect of himself but for the purposes of God; God therefore has a first call on his property." It is required that "every man afford his help to another in every want or distress [...] Community of perils calls for extraordinary liberality, and so doth community in some special service for the church." "He is worse than an Infidel who through his own sloth and voluptuousness shall neglect to provide for his family." In case of community of perils, one must act "with more enlargement towards others, and less respect towards ourselves and our own right." The group was to:

> seek out a place of cohabitation and consortship under a due form of government both civil and ecclesiastical. In such cases as this, the care of the public must over-sway all private respects [...] we must be willing to abridge ourselves of our superfluities for the supply of others' necessities, we must delight in each other, mourn together, labour and suffer together, always having before our eyes our Commission and Community in the work [...] we must consider that we shall be as a City upon a Hill. The eyes of all people are upon us [...] we shall be made a story and a byword throughout the world.[12]

It was said of this that it was "the most intense community experience of modern times [...] In the absence of true communities we would have witnessed the re-creation of European peasants and landlords."[13] What resulted was said to be a:

self-sustaining colony three thousand miles away from bishops and king [...] the most radical government in the European world: a republic, where the Puritan men elected their governor, deputy governor and legislature (known as the General Court) [...] the healthiest, the most populous and the most egalitarian in the distribution of property [...] New English leaders favored relatively compact settlement in towns to concentrate people sufficiently for defense, to support public schools, to promote mutual supervision of morality and above all to sustain a convenient and well-attended local church [...] commitment to a moral, educated, commercial and homogeneous people.[14]

It has been observed that each of the chartered American colonies was a good advertisement for non-prescriptive chartering of new institutions:

All the early settlements were conducted by private enterprise under distant and irregular state supervision; this was another case of "self-government by the King's command." The first contested election in the New World was held as early as 1637, without any reference to the English government [...] 150 years of devising their own institutions.[15]

An "Essay on the Ordering of Towns," undated but prepared in 1635, proposed towns each six miles square with a meeting-house at the center. Its premise was declared to be that "one acre enclosed is much more beneficial than five in common."[16] A General Act for the Incorporation of Towns was enacted in 1635, the first American general incorporation law. According to Adrian and Griffith:

No borough corporations were established in the chartered colonies of Massachusetts, Connecticut, and Rhode Island. The characteristic "town" incorporations were issued under the authority of the assemblies within a few years of settlement. Some towns claimed (and apparently successfully) their corporate rights through long-established usage. Differences of opinion as to their precise corporate nature still exist.[17]

In February 1636 the church in Boston renewed its covenant among members whereby they agreed "to keep ourselves pure from the sins of the times."[18]

The colony had begun with the transplantation of a community from England; communities led by their pastors were to be further transplanted to western New York, Ohio, and points further west. Tocqueville was to observe that "The township of Ohio is very analogous to the township of Massachusetts."[19]

A group that wished to establish a new town in Massachusetts needed the permission of the colony's legislature. When the legislature approved a request, its franchise not only conferred the right to create a government for a new town and the right to send representatives to the legislature but also carried title to an allotment of land. This land was legally deeded to a group of leaders or proprietors of the planned settlement. These leaders distributed the land, to themselves as well as others, according to a number of criteria, including social status, family size and extent of investment in the colony. In each town much of the land was initially not distributed but was held out for common use and grants to later settlers as well as for later division among the original proprietors when the growth of their families made larger landholdings advantageous. The leaders who owned the town's land were among the initial voting membership of the town's political meeting and made up an important part of the members of the town's covenanted church.[20]

Winthrop's first decisive judgment was to specify that the meetings of the proprietors of the new colony were to take place in the New World, thus emancipating the colony from absentee control and enabling it to be adjusted to circumstances by those who had knowledge of its conditions. Some 15,000 to 20,000 immigrants were attracted in the first ten years. The moral law was enforced by forbidding all persons from living alone and requiring literacy and church attendance of all. Separatism was discouraged so as not to anger the crown. The drinking of toasts was forbidden as an aid to temperance. Persons were "sifted" before being allowed to sign the church covenant; church membership was a condition of the political franchise, initially accorded to less than 10 percent of the population.[21] Each individual congregation could determine its own affairs, a principle confirmed as the Cambridge Platform by a convention of churches in 1648 which still defines Congregationalist practice. Church services customarily lasted all day Sunday, with sermons in both the morning and afternoon and questions from the congregation about points of doctrine.[22] Recalcitrants were "reasoned with" by the leaders of the community. The freemen assembled four times a year and elected a governor and 18 assistants for annual terms; the assistants and governor met monthly; "government was in the nature of a parliament." Ministers were excluded from public office. Freemen came to be chosen on a religious basis and not for payment of shares.

The governor's authority was substantially absolute, save for annually renewable consent: "a despotism with all the efficiencies of despotism." Initially, the assistants were elected at large by all the voters. In 1632 the election of governors was transferred from the assistants to the freemen. Initially, the freemen had no legislative powers; in 1634, however, they gained power over taxation and land distribution, and the power to make laws and elect officers. The General Court was authorized to meet four times a year, rather than twice; each town could send delegates, and sessions could not be ended without majority consent. For the first time, Winthrop was required to relinquish the governorship.

In 1636, the Court of Assistants began being localized to each town and towns were authorized to dispose of their own lands and to choose their own constables and surveyors. They began to be used to collect taxes, organize the militia, maintain highways, supply juries, and register vital statistics. Contrary to Winthrop's preference, the view was taken that "strict discipline both in criminal offenses and in martial affairs was more needed on plantations than in a settled state."[23] Magistrates were to sit in pairs but speak with one voice.

There were seven towns by 1630 and 20 by 1640.[24] There was no lord lieutenant, rather a decentralized militia for which the assistants appointed officers and made rules; later the militias were allowed to nominate their officers, subject to approval by the magistrates. No appeals to England were allowed. There were no manors or manorial courts like those in Carolina, Maryland, and New York, and no hereditary element in the working constitution. In 1639, the council of assistants was restructured, and the assistants elected by towns rather than at large. Another innovation was "the New England Confederation, the league of Bible communities of which Winthrop was an architect," established in 1643.[25] The Confederation provided for common defense, arbitration of disputes, and return of runaways and fleeing criminals. Despite its short life, it recognized "a [federal] principle of inestimable benefit to their state."[26] In 1639, a *Body of Liberties* was proclaimed (codified in 1648), prohibiting monopolies and restraints on alienation of land and providing for trial by jury and the organization of towns, and providing for humane treatment of debtors who were permitted to satisfy debts by payment in kind or transfers of goods without forced sales.[27] It also included rudimentary guarantees of free speech and assembly ("every man whether inhabitant or foreigner free or not free" can speak), a right of exit, and criminal procedure guarantees including bail and freedom from torture, together with debtors' exemptions going beyond those in English law.[28] Its eloquent preamble began:

> No man's life shall be taken away; no man's honour or good name shall be stained; no man's person shall be arrested, restrained, banished, dismembered nor in any way punished; no man shall be deprived of his wife or children; no man's goods or estate shall be taken away from him nor any way damaged under colour of law or countenance of authority unless it be by virtue of some express law of the county warranting the same, established by a general court and sufficiently published.[29]

Punishments were largely swift and corporal, involving public humiliation through branding, whipping, or confinement in stocks or pillories.[30]

It has been urged by a late-nineteenth-century writer, Asa Eaton, that the *Body of Liberties* declared inherent rights of local self-government like those recognized in section 16 of the Magna Carta:

And the City of London shall have all its convenient liberties and its free customs as well by land as by water. Furthermore we will and grant that all other cities, burghs and towns and ports shall have all their liberties and free customs.[31]

While the Supreme Court ultimately rejected claims of an inherent right of local self-government in *Hunter v. City of Pittsburgh*,[32] nearly all states have subsequently adopted municipal home rule amendments to their state constitutions that strikingly resemble the right that Eaton defined as constitutionally protected:

the right to govern ourselves in all matters of local concern free from the control of the legislature except through general laws applicable to all such units alike or through particular laws passed at the request and with the consent of such units.[33]

Tocqueville wrote of the New England township:

The institutions of a township are to freedom what primary schools are to science [...] they put it within reach of the people [...] without the institutions of a township a nation can give itself a free government but it does not have the spirit of freedom. Political life was born in the very bosom of the townships; one can almost say that each of them at its origin was an independent power [...] [I]t was they that seemed to relinquish a portion of their independence in favour of the state.[34]

Section 66 of the *Body of Liberties* allowed towns to enact general civil regulations, "not criminal but prudential," with a maximum fine of 20 shillings; these related to "that large class of miscellaneous subjects affecting the accommodation and convenience of the inhabitants which have been placed under the municipal jurisdiction of towns by statute or by usage."[35] In this course of development Winthrop and his colleagues displayed "keen political sense in knowing when and how far to yield power [...] to compromise their dearest convictions if only government might go on."[36] Adjudication of offenses was not ceded to popular control; Winthrop strongly objected to "referring matters of counsel or judicature to the body of the people."[37]

Winthrop unsuccessfully argued against a criminal code based on Mosaic Law adopted in 1641. In his view, the justice of the magistrate was to be informed by discretion:

> All punishments ought to be just, and offenses varying so much in their merit by occasion of circumstances, it would be unjust to inflict the same punishment upon the least as upon the greatest [...] Justice requires that every cause shall be heard before it be judged which cannot be when the sentence and punishment is determined before-hand. God hath not confined all wisdom, etc. to any one generation that they should set rules for all others.[38]

In 1647, important rights were conceded in recognition of "useful parts and abilities of diverse inhabitants among us who are not freemen," who were permitted to serve on town boards provided they did not make up a majority of a board and were 24 years of age and without criminal convictions.[39]

In 1642, what amounted to a compulsory education law was adopted, requiring parents to teach their children to read and understand the principles of religion and the laws of the colony. Later, each town of 50 or more families was required to hire a schoolmaster, and in 1647 towns of 100 or more families were required to hire a teacher of Latin grammar. In 1645, in response to parliamentary ascendancy in England, the franchise in towns was extended.[40] According to Parrington:

> In the Bible commonwealth, the legislative function was regarded as of minor importance. The law being already set out in the Scriptures, the chief authority in the commonwealth naturally rested with the magistrates who were responsible for its strict fulfilment [...], absolute legislative and judicial powers.[41]

The governor and assistants could veto any requests of the free-men; "the old English right of petition in short was not a right in theocratic Massachusetts," though Winthrop declared, "we hope we shall be willing (by God's assistance) to hearken to good advice from any of you."[42] To deny the veto, Winthrop said in 1643, would be "to establish a meere Democratie," failing to preserve the people from their violent passions.[43] In 1644, the assistants and deputies were required to separately concur in all legislation; the beginnings of bicameralism.[44] Harmony was preserved through the secession and/or expulsion of dissidents, a valuable safety valve availed of by such people as Roger Williams and Anne Hutchinson.[45] Yet Winthrop remained a friend of Roger Williams, who acknowledged that "you bear with fools gladly, because you are wise."[46]

On similar principles, free immigration was not permitted; in May 1637, Winthrop declared that:

> the nature of [...] incorporation ties every member thereof to seek out and entertain all means that may conduce to the welfare of the body and to keep off whatever appears to tend to their damage. We may lawfully refuse to receive such whose dispositions suit not with ours and whose society we know will be harmful to us. We are not bound to exercise mercy to others to the ruin of ourselves. A family is a little commonwealth and a commonwealth is a great family. Now as a family is not bound to entertain all comers, not even every good man (other than by way of hospitality), no more is a commonwealth.[47]

Strangers were limited to a stay of 14 days in a town, unless a longer stay was approved by town officers.[48]

The towns functioned essentially as closed corporations. Initially, some lots were saved for newcomers. Thereafter they parceled out all land among their members, and increasingly provided tax loopholes for non-resident owners.[49] Winthrop sought to limit land grants in order to preserve a class of landless tradesmen, who would otherwise demand excessive wages. In Winthrop's conception, "every man must love his brother, in the sense of not attempting to change places but of achieving the welfare of the corporate or organic whole by performing to the full the place or function assigned him."[50] In 1684, the original charter was revoked by the English courts, and rule by an English governor general was established. In 1691, a new charter expressly conferred liberty of conscience, an end to quit-rents, and local control over taxing and spending, later impairment of which was one of the causes of the American Revolution.[51]

Ultimately, in Massachusetts as elsewhere, "every colony based its representation in the colonial assembly on local units."[52] These ultimately bore only limited resemblance to Winthrop's "covenanted community," though deriving from it. According to Rutman, "He envisioned a society in which men would subordinate themselves to their brothers' and the community's good, but he sought to erect that society in a land where opportunity for individual profit lay ready to every hand."[53]

> Within this fragmented society, where long-established relationships were non-existent, where families were disrupted, where the church itself was a divisive element, where materialism and individualism were tending toward social chaos, only the secular authority—the political organization of society—could unite, could define the relationship of one individual to another.[54]

This system was destroyed in the twentieth-century era of legislative reapportionment, leading to "Neighbourhoods of strangers and jurisdictions without traditions."[55] It was said of the New England town that "The failure to grasp it and to continue it, indeed to incorporate it in both the federal and state constitutions was one of the tragic oversights of post-revolutionary political development."[56] Tocqueville for his part observed: "where the town system is not the base, therefore the expenditure of the legislature is not economic but prodigal." James Bryce observed:

> Not a little of that robust, if narrow, localism which characterizes the representative system of America is due to this originally distinct and corporate life of the seventeenth century towns. Nor is it without interest to observe that although they owed much to the conditions which surrounded the early colonists, forcing them to develop a civic patriotism resembling that of the republics of ancient Greece and Italy, they owed something also to those Teutonic traditions of semi-independent local communities owning common property and governed by a primary assembly of all free inhabitants which the English

had brought with them from the Elbe and the Weser and which had been perpetuated in the practice of many parts of England down till the days of the Stuart kings.[57]

Winthrop's heritage was said to be "the widest colonial franchise […] a history of congregational autonomy in the churches […] and above all town meetings [resulting in] the best ordered, the least levelled, the most deferential part of American society."[58] "In New England […] the common people are accustomed to respect intellectual and moral superiority and to submit to it without complaint."[59]

3

Thomas Jefferson and the Midwestern Township

The Northwest Ordinance was the first and perhaps the greatest statute enacted by the Congress that was newly created in 1787. It re-enacted without substantial changes the last major statute of the Continental Congress functioning under the Articles of Confederation. The statute provided for the organization of the lands that became the states of Ohio, Indiana, Illinois, Michigan, and Wisconsin. It was not a perfect law, nor a long one, but much thought had been given to it. Its earliest antecedent was Jefferson's stillborn draft constitution for Virginia drawn up in 1776, a productive year for Jefferson. That draft constitution occupied ten pages, exclusive of its recitals;[1] at the time it was drawn up, Virginia was the principal claimant to the Western lands which, when ceded to the United States, made up the Northwest Territory. Four paragraphs of that instrument helped define the future character of the American Midwest:

> Un-appropriated or forfeited lands shall be appropriated by the Administrator with the consent of the Privy Council. Every person of full age neither owning nor having owned 50 acres of land shall be entitled to an appropriation of fifty acres or to so much as shall make up what he owns or has owned fifty acres in full and absolute dominion. And no other persons shall be capable of taking an appropriation.

5. Thomas Jefferson (Library of Congress)

No land shall be appropriated until purchased of the Indian nation proprietors; nor shall any purchases be made of them but on behalf of the public, by authority of acts of the General Assembly to be passed for every purchase specially.

The Western and Northern extent of this [State] shall in all [...] respects stand as fixed until by act of the legislature one or more territories shall be laid off Westward of the Alleghany [*sic*] mountains for new colonies, which colonies shall be established on the same fundamental laws contained in this instrument, and shall be free and independent of this colony and of all the world.

No person hereafter coming into this county [i.e. west of the Alleghenies] shall be held within the same in slavery under any pretext whatsoever.

The principles here outlined—that Native American country was to initially become public land, that the future nation was to consist of equal states and not colonies, and that slavery was to be

6. Thomas Jefferson, founder of the University of
Virginia, Charlottesville, Virginia

excluded from the West—defined the subject-matter of American politics for the ensuing 75 years.

Also in 1776, Jefferson attempted to add to the provision of the Articles of Confederation promising full membership to Canada a proviso extending it to "all new colonies to be established by the United States," and further providing that "land when purchased shall be given freely to those who may be permitted to seat them."[2]

In 1780, the Continental Congress, prior to ratifying the Articles of Confederation, adopted a resolution calling for state surrender of lands, declaring a purpose to form them into "distinct republican states, which shall become members of the Federal Union and shall have the same rights of sovereignty, freedom and independence as the other states." In James

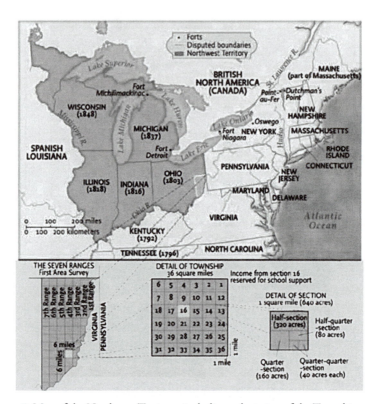

7. Map of the Northwest Territory, including a depiction of the Township system (www.americanhistoryusa.com)

Willard Hurst's words: "We knew better than to adopt a doctrinaire individualism [...] the procedure best known through the Northwest Ordinance of 1787 for orderly creation of new states out of a wilderness [...] pertained to the deliberate making of public order."[3]

In 1784, Jefferson was chairman of a committee of the Continental Congress on the Western Lands that likewise provided for the creation of new states. The statute would have allowed existing settlers to establish temporary governments adopting the constitution of an existing state, to call constitutional conventions when they reached a population of 20,000, and to be admitted as a state when attaining a population of

60,000.[4] Jefferson also proposed a ban on slavery after the year 1800 "in any of the said states," after further providing that the law was to apply to "the territory ceded or to be ceded by individual states to the United States," not merely to the Northwest Territory. The 1784 law was enacted but never implemented. It was drafted as a compact between states, a fact that became important when its successor, the Northwest Ordinance of 1787, was tested in the Supreme Court.[5] The anti-slavery proposal failed by one vote, leading Jefferson to declare that "the fate of millions unborn" hung "on the tongue of one man, and heaven was silent at that awful moment."[6]

In the course of enactment, the 1784 act was amended to forbid discrimination against non-resident property owners in taxation, a measure sought by land speculators, and to forbid state taxation of federal lands. Congress also was suspicious of the adventurers and hunter-gatherers who were the first entrants into the new territories. It therefore provided that the temporary government which gave settlers virtually all the rights of states save representation in Congress would not be formed until land was "offered for sale,"[7] and empowered Congress in the meantime to adopt measures "necessary for the preservation of peace and good order."[8]

A week after the adoption of the 1784 ordinance, another committee under Jefferson presented a report on the Establishment of a Land Office.[9] This also was a seminal document. It provided for the surveying and laying out of the new territories in rectangular grids, each of 100 square miles, subdivided into one-mile tracts, thus avoiding the title problems attendant to the development of Virginia, where tracts had irregular and frequently conflicting boundaries. It also provided for the sale of land at a uniform price per acre. In lieu of homestead provisions, and pursuant to an agreement between Jefferson and Hamilton, the proceeds of sales were to be applied "to the sinking of the national debt, and to no other purpose whatsoever." Jefferson would have liked to go further; in the same year, he wrote James Madison's father to declare that "it is not too soon to provide by every possible means that as few as possible shall be without a little portion of land. The small landholders are the most precious part of the state."[10] War veterans were to receive warrants to be applied to sale prices. Another committee under Jefferson called for the cession by the states of their western land claims.[11] The land office measure was amended to reduce the platted grids to 36 square miles in area, the area of New England townships, and to provide that un-surveyed land could not be sold; this promoted a gradual westward movement and greater concentration of the population. One lot in each township was reserved for schools and four for future sale; an intermediate variation would have provided for 49-square-mile tracts and the allocation of one block to religious institutions.

Jefferson's original design for "ward government" contemplated three years of free education in primary schools of 40 students, each erected by taxation or compelled labor by a ward of five or six square miles with a population of about 500:

> At every of those schools shall be taught reading, writing and common arithmetic and the books which will be used therein for teaching children to read shall be such as will at the same time make them acquainted with Grecian, Roman, English and American history. History [...] will enable them to know ambition under whatever guise it may assume, and, knowing it, to defeat its views.[12]

By 1787, Congress had second thoughts about the 1784 ordinance with what were thought to be its excessive rights for early settlers. A draft statute provided for a conventional colonial government until a new state acquired 60,000 persons. Jefferson, then in Paris, cautioned that "To treat settlers as subjects" would cause them to "abhor us as masters and break from us in defiance."[13] He urged small states, at one point presenting a map dividing the territory into 14 states, although the 1784 ordinance provided for only six.[14] He considered that settlers "will not only be happier in a state of moderate size, but it is the only way in which they can exist as a regular society."[15] "A state of such extent as 160,000 square miles would soon crumble into little ones" (a prophecy of some relevance to today's California and Texas), or, as he had earlier said in his *Notes on Virginia*: "great societies cannot exist without government—therefore break them into little ones." The 1787 act was passed during Jefferson's absence in Europe and partially accommodated his views; it provided for a territorial legislature when a state population reached 5,000, the congressionally appointed governor retaining a veto, and for statehood, subject to approval of Congress, when a population of 60,000 was reached. Alternate townships were to be sold as units, an important provision that promoted the migration of whole townships of people from New England, frequently led by their pastors.[16] A price of $1.00 per acre was provided for; the homestead ideal was partially accommodated by allowing one year's credit on half the purchase price. The acts of Congress admitting Ohio and each of the 21 new states admitted before the Civil War, except for Vermont, Kentucky, Maine, and Texas, also provided that in each state "not more than two complete townships [were] to be given perpetually for the purposes of a university," leading to the creation of 17 state universities by the time of the Civil War. The provisions of land for this purpose fulfilled the general admonition in the 1787 ordinance that "religion, morality and knowledge being necessary to good government and the happiness of mankind, schools and the means of education shall forever be encouraged." A total of 60 million acres went to public schools and 4 million to universities. Jefferson observed that if the new governments "can be retained til their governments become settled and wise, they will be with us always."[17]

In 1790, he protested an attempt at lawmaking by a governor,[18] leading President Washington to send a private admonition to the governor.[19]

The 1787 Northwest Ordinance barred slavery from the newly organized territory but not from other territory "ceded or to be ceded" to the United States. The sectional line it defined excited Jefferson's increasing abhorrence. Historian Roger Kennedy, in his *Mr. Jefferson's Lost Cause: Slavery and the Louisiana Purchase* (2003), pointed out that Jefferson made no effort to secure prohibitions of slavery in the congressional acts admitting Kentucky and Tennessee to the union in 1792 and 1796, nor in the act establishing Mississippi Territory in 1798. The 1803 bill relating to the newly acquired Louisiana Territory, like that relating to Mississippi, limited itself to a ban on the importation of slaves from abroad or from South Carolina, the only state that still allowed importation. The biographer Merrill Peterson takes a different view than Kennedy of Jefferson's failure to seek to ban slavery in Louisiana:

> Realistically, he could do no more. To lock up this rich country to slaves, to prohibit southern planters from migrating there, to force the territory into an economic pattern alien to itself and its neighbors—Jefferson never even considered these propositions [...] Lower Louisiana was not very promising ground on which to test the federal power to restrict slavery in the territories.[20]

With the effectiveness of the prohibition of slave imports in 1808, Jefferson abandoned any interest he may previously have had in limiting the area in which slavery was illegal. Some have taken the view that the opposition by Jefferson and Madison to the Missouri Compromise in 1820 was founded on a desire to preserve the veto of the Southern states in the Senate and to sustain agricultural interests, including planter interests, against those of manufacturing. Jefferson has been reproached for disliking manufacturers more than he disliked slavery. The counter-argument is that Jefferson was consistent in favoring national uniformity; the evil to be avoided was a geographic demarcation line that would foster disunity. "That line once conceived I feared would never be obliterated from the mind."[21] Allied to this were two other convictions: a belief in the equality and self-government of states, and a conviction that once imports of slaves had been shut off, slavery could best be dealt with as a national problem.

In 1820, Jefferson wrote Lafayette, saying:

> All know that permitting the slaves of the South to spread into the West will not add one being to that unfortunate condition [but] will increase the happiness [of slaves] and by spreading them over a larger surface will dilute the evil everywhere and facilitate the means of getting finally rid of it, an event more anxiously wished by those on whom it presses than by the noisy pretenders to exclusive humanity.[22]

Dispersion would "divide the burden on a greater number of co-adjustors."

Whether or not this was reasonable in 1820, it did not appear so by 1850. By the time of the Civil War, slavery was a dying institution in the Upper South; 80 percent of the slaves in Delaware were free as well as 50 percent of those in Maryland and upwards of 20 percent of those in Virginia.[23] Slavery was preserved by the sale of slaves to the south-western territories where their use was economic.

The heir to Jefferson's view was Stephen A. Douglas, whose attachment to territorial self-government manifested itself with respect to issues other than slavery, as the historian Richard Johannsen has demonstrated.[24] It was Douglas, following Jefferson, who viewed slavery as a municipal matter and upheld what the fair-minded historian Peter Onuf has called "the claims of state equality, self-constitution and non-interference."[25]

Jefferson proved to be right about the fateful nature of the vote in 1784. Many thought that the ban on importation of slaves after 1808 doomed slavery, but Madison, at the Constitutional Convention, thought otherwise: the 20-year grace period would solidify the institution. Jefferson in his 1806 annual message to Congress successfully urged enforcement of the ban on importation.[26]

If Jefferson's anti-slavery initiative failed, his homestead proposal had a happier fate. Sales of public land in the first years after the Northwest Ordinance were modest, at about 1 million acres per year. Almost from the enactment of the Northwest Ordinance, efforts were made through special "pre-emption" acts to give settlers already on the land a preferential position at land sales. By 1820, 24 special acts containing such privileges had been enacted; about 3 percent of the land went to buyers claiming under pre-emption. In 1830, Congress enacted a general pre-emption act signed by President Jackson. Under it, pre-emptions markedly increased; in 1831, they accounted for 20 percent of land sales. In 1835 and 1836, there was a frenzy of land speculation encouraged by loose credit on the part of banks, which caused annual land sales to explode to more than 15 million acres (25,000 square miles) in 1835 and 20 million acres in 1836. This led to Jackson's specie circular of 1836 requiring all land purchasers other than settlers to pay in gold or silver, settlers being given the privilege of using banknotes for a year. Jackson's avowed purpose was "to save the new states from a non-resident proprietorship, one of the greatest obstacles to advancement of a new country and the prosperity of an old one." The specie circular caused speculative land sales to drop to a fourth of the previous levels.[27]

Presidents Pierce and Buchanan, under the pressure of Southern planters and speculators, limited squatter rights to one year, thus discouraging pre-emption and building pressure for a homestead law. Such laws were sponsored throughout the 1850s with the support of Horace Greeley, the most influential newspaper publisher of the time; one passed the House in 1858, and in 1859 Buchanan used his veto against another such proposal, one that had been watered down to escape his veto by providing the right to buy 160 acres after five years' occupancy for 25 cents per acre. The unexpected veto helped discredit the Douglas Democrats in the North, and thus contributed to the victory of Lincoln and the Republicans.[28]

Despite controversies over slavery, Congress kept its promise in the Northwest Ordinance by admitting states not too long after they achieved the requisite population and sometimes before they had reached that point. Ohio was admitted in 1803. Indiana, which was shown by a special census to have 63,897 white males of age in 1815, was admitted in the following year. The population of Illinois in December 1818 was 40,258 and it was admitted shortly thereafter. A Michigan census showed a population of 85,856 in 1834; the state was admitted in 1837. The admission of Wisconsin had been delayed by boundary disputes; it had the very large population of 280,000 when it entered the Union. The same principle was ultimately applied to all the states in the continental United States, in some instances with time delays due to the slavery or other controversies. Even Louisiana, with a foreign legal system, was admitted eight years after the Louisiana Purchase, lending force to a prophecy in Jefferson's Second Inaugural Address: "Who can limit the extent to which the federative principle may operate effectively?"[29] The only limits encountered were those enforced with respect to the insular territories acquired in the Spanish–American War of 1898, and then only after fierce criticism on the basis of Jeffersonian principles from Speaker Thomas Reed and other anti-imperialists.

The 1785 Land Office Ordinance likewise had large effects. The Western states were spared by grid mapping from the title controversies and overlapping claims of the Atlantic seaboard states, and the provision for platting and grant of land in townships redressed, for the Northwest Territory at least, the absence of any provisions for or references to local government in the federal constitution.[30] Taken in all, the Northwest Ordinance and Land Office Ordinance did succeed in "proliferating purposes"; their provisions for virtually automatic organization of self-government captured the public's imagination and influenced the nation's territorial expansion for more than a century. The attempts to territorially restrict slavery, put forward at a time when slavery persisted in Europe and even in the Northern states, set in motion forces outrunning the desires of those who launched them; and the broaching of the prospect of free land and government sales of it at low fixed prices bore fruit in later public policy and reverberated not only in American politics but in the consciousness of the peoples of Europe.

It has been said that "Jefferson's therapeutic view of land won its proudest victory over a purely commodity theory of land in the Homestead Act."[31] Even before its enactment in 1862, its theory had been reflected in the pre-emption laws and in the government's willingness, in a period of rising population and growing demand for land, to sell land at constant or falling per-acre prices and in smaller and smaller lots. Tocqueville had thus been able to write in 1835 that the "lands of the New World belong to the first occupant; they are the natural reward of the swiftest pioneer."[32] Like most successful legislation, the Homestead Act built upon established values. The price of $2 per acre fixed by the Federalists in 1790, half of which was to be in cash, was maintained for 20 years, but the minimum unit of purchase was reduced from 640 acres in 1790 to 320 acres in 1800, to 160 acres in 1804 and to 80 acres in 1820. In that year, credit sales were abolished but the price was lowered to $1.25 per acre. The minimum lot size was reduced to 40 acres in 1832, making it possible to buy a tract of land for $50.

The Homestead Act accorded any head of household the right to own 160 acres of public land by registering his entry and residing on and improving it for five years. Alternatively the settler could acquire the land six months after entry for $1.25 per acre. Paul W. Gates of Cornell University, who is almost certainly the leading academic authority on American public land, observed of the Homestead Acts that "their noble purpose and the great part they played in enabling nearly a million and a half people to acquire farm land, much of which developed into farm homes, far outweigh the misuse to which they were put."[33]

The Homestead Act operated in parallel to continuing land sales by the government as well as by railroads and state governments. During the period 1863–70, the land entered under the Homestead Act totaled about 5 million acres, or 8,000 square miles; the lands sold totaled somewhat more than 6 million acres (10,000 square miles). As Hurst observed, nineteenth-century Congresses "used the national public domain as a substitute for cash" and yielded to "settlers' pressure and the broad public opinion favouring promotional use of the lands."[34]

The initial Homestead Act of 1862 was followed by a Southern Homestead Act in 1866 applicable to the five Southern states in which there were significant amounts of public land, namely Alabama, Arkansas, Florida, Louisiana, and Mississippi. Congressman George Julian, a former abolitionist, was one of a small group in Congress that had secured two wartime acts of Congress providing for the confiscation of the estates of rebel planters. He unsuccessfully sought the division of these plantations into 40-acre tracts to be given to the freedmen and the reservation of remaining public lands for homestead applicants. The act, when passed, contained no special provisions for the freedmen, let alone any cash grants to assist them in making improvements, and provided a minimum unit of entry of 80 acres for the first two years. The available land was for the most part not agricultural land, most of which had been sold earlier, but refuse land and, according to Gates, "an abundance of relatively infertile land covered with heavy stands of longleaf pine and cyprus."

It is significant that Northern lumber interests supported the bill, whether to eliminate potential competition or to obtain land for themselves through questionable entries.

There were about 62,000 entries covering about 6.4 million acres, or 10,000 square miles, in the ten years the Southern Homestead Act was in operation. Somewhere between a fifth and a third of the entries were carried to patent; with respect to many of them, the entry lasted only until the timber was stripped off. The roughly 28,000 final entries, nearly half of them in Arkansas, represented about 6 percent of the land that was offered; in Mississippi, about 23 percent of the patentees were African-American, suggesting that not more than about 6,000 African-Americans benefited from the law, which was repealed in 1876 and was characterized as "a mere gesture in the right direction."[35]

Similar problems existed with respect to grants of the dry land west of the 100th meridian fostered by the 1873 Timber Culture Act and the 1877 Desert Land Act. Subsequent to repeal of the Southern Homestead Act, there were large sales of public land to timber companies, though homesteading was still available on 160-acre tracts under the general homestead law.

In 1891, Congress finally enacted a comprehensive reform, which curtailed land sales, repealed the Timber Culture and pre-emption acts, tightened the Desert Land Act, and denied the right of homestead to persons owning more than 160 acres. By this time, most worthwhile public land had been distributed or sold, but the Commissioner of the Public Land Office could finally declare that "The great object of the government is to dispose of the public lands to actual settlers only—to bona fide tillers of the soil."[36]

In 1904, in an effort to recognize the uneconomic nature of 160-acre tracts beyond the 100th parallel, Congress passed the Kincaid Act, applicable to Western Nebraska only, allowing acquisition of 640-acre tracts in semi-arid lands. Administration of the act was shot through with fraud, the tracts generally winding up with large cattle ranchers. The effect, as described by Professor Harold Hedges, was that "Fenced pastures have replaced the open range and private control of the land is the rule. The final result is a cattle industry established on a much sounder basis than in the days of free grass."[37]

In 1909, after much misleading propaganda by land companies on the alleged ease of "dry farming," Congress passed the Enlarged Homestead Act allowing grants of 320-acre tracts on non-irrigable, non-mineral land having no merchantable timber in nine Western states, extended to four others by separate acts in 1910, 1912, and 1915. The land almost invariably passed into the hands of large cattle ranchers. In 1916, the Stock Raising Homestead Act was enacted, providing for 640-acre grants; like its predecessor, it purported to require the homesteader to make permanent improvements, such as fencing and wells, equal to $1.25 per acre. There were 25,000 entries under the act in 1921 and from 5,000 to 7,000 annually until 1934. A representative of the Forest Service pointed out that the remaining public lands were "remnant lands," that it would take 35 to 50 acres of such land to keep a cow, that not one tract in 1,000 had surface water, and that well drilling was generally fruitless. The need to acquire homesteads that would otherwise be open range burdened ranchers. It was estimated in 1956 that about 80,000 square miles or 50 million acres had gone to private ownership under the enlarged Homestead and Stock Raising Homestead Acts and that about three-fourths of this area had been rendered useless for grazing unless re-seeded.

In 1934, with the enactment of the Taylor Grazing Act, lands included in grazing districts were withdrawn from entry under any of the Homestead Acts except land subsequently found to be more valuable for agricultural crops than native grasses, which would be homesteaded in 320-acre tracts. Existing rights prior to the enactment were saved. As a result, the number of final entries under the Homestead Acts fell to a few hundred a year in the 1940s; in 1966, there were 196 final entries totaling 23,405 acres and 51 original entries totaling 7,442 acres, 95–98 percent of which were in Alaska. In April 1945, virtually coincident with President Roosevelt's death, Secretary of the Interior Ickes made an extravagant proposal for 415 new irrigation projects, to cost $5 billion, on which 400,000 veterans were to be settled. This came to naught as a result of rising environmentalist opposition to new dam projects. In the 20 years after World War II the Bureau of Reclamation constructed 110 new dams at a cost of $1.6 billion, but only 3,041 new farms were created.[38]

It remained true, in the words of Paul W. Gates, that the fact that:

> 1,322,107 homesteaders carried their entries to final patent after three to five years of residence is overwhelming evidence that despite the poorly framed legislation with its invitation to fraud, the Homestead Law was the successful route to farm ownership of the great majority of settlers moving into the newer areas of the West after 1862.[39]

The essence of the Homestead Act, when properly administered, was the unification of the government's land and the settler's labor. In the states of the Northwest Territory, it was estimated that it required a month's labor and the services of a team of oxen to clear an acre of land. The costs of clearing woodland were estimated by the scholar Martin Primack at $10–12 per acre and the costs of clearing prairie at $3–5.[40] In 1860, the Minnesota Commissioner of Statistics advised would-be settlers that in addition to land, they would require $200 for house furniture and provisions until they became self-sustaining, $100 to build a house, $150 for a team of horses and a wagon, $60 for special labor and equipment to clear original prairie, $45 for tools, and $40 for two cows, a total of $595, or a year-and-a-half's wage for the average worker in 1860.[41] These statistics sufficiently illustrate why the Southern Homestead Act, without more, was of little use to the ex-slaves.

Only about 40 percent of the original entries under the Homestead Act were finalized, a statistic that concealed much disappointment. In addition, the act was criticized for establishing minimum rather than maximum acreages and encouraging speculation and concentration of ownership by reason of the lack of restrictions on alienation of land. It has been charged with promoting the settlement of the West "too early."[42] On the other hand, the attractions of homesteading and the speculation in land that its loose administration and federal land sales and land grants invited were a stimulus to migration and immigration. The law by itself was well-known and provided incentives; it was supplemented by the promotional efforts of speculators and of railroads receiving land grants; several Midwestern states sent

Immigration Commissioners to Europe to recruit new citizens. The end result, as the contributors to the relevant chapter in the *Cambridge Economic History of the United States* have noted, was that "In less than half a century, wilderness was converted into one of the world's great agricultural regions."[43] There are lessons in this for our perverse immigration policies, which divorce rights from responsibilities and extend few rewards to either labor or investment.

4

Albert Gallatin and Municipal Enterprise

American local government today is distinguished by a plethora of local authorities and special taxing districts. These are considered a mixed blessing. At their best, they are optimally designed for economies of scale with respect to the services that they render. The canton of Vaud in Switzerland, a place of pilgrimage for public choice theorists, has carried this approach to its extreme. The general cantonal government does almost nothing. All public services are performed by districts of varying sizes, each sized according to economies of scale. The special district is frequently a means of uniting and raising public and private capital, and avoiding the tendencies toward extravagance that sometimes arise in jurisdictions where universal suffrage coexists with a non-property-owning majority. Special districts with a property rather than personal franchise are thus attractive to fiscal conservatives. On the other hand, at their worst, they lack both democratic and market accountability, have opaque finances, are subject to conflicts of interest and unclear fiduciary standards, and can lead to the corruption that once led Felix Frankfurter to observe that he believed in capitalism, and in regulated capitalism, but not in state capitalism.

But such arrangements have played a large part in American history. As stated by Leonard D. White,[1]

8. Portrait of Albert Gallatin by Gilbert Stuart, c. 1803 (Public domain)

the mixed corporation was the favored device for financing those internal improvements, recommended by Gallatin[2] and employed by both the federal and state governments [...] In the major public improvements there was some sentiment that the public interest was best served by full governmental responsibility.[3]

At a later time, Franklin D. Roosevelt:

pointed out the benefits of the districts as a way to avoid municipal defaults [...] [I]n 1934, he sent a letter to governors urging them to create public corporations that could issue revenue bonds. He urged the creation of water, sewer and electric light and power districts [...] He also dispensed model enabling legislation for housing authorities and soil conservation districts.[4]

9. North facade of 1823 stone house, with 1895 dining room at right.
Friendship Hill, 223 New Geneva Road, Point Marion, Fayette County, PA
(Library of Congress)

As was noted by an early-twentieth-century political scientist,
Thomas Reed, "The seventeenth and eighteenth century municipality existed for corporate rather than governmental purposes—
management of corporate property and the protection of corporate
trade privileges."[5]

Private corporations had limited functions in the early years
of the Republic:

incorporation required a special act of the legislature. At that time,
the grant of a corporate charter conferred quasi-governmental
powers on the organizers, and hence was restricted to groups that
undertook to perform vital public services—for example, building
a bridge or a road to improve transportation routes, or organiz-
ing a bank to provide the community with a circulating medium
and source of credit. In exchange for providing such services, the

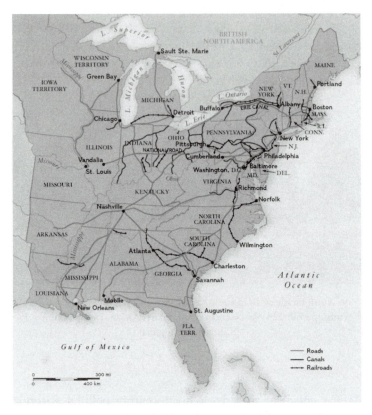

10. Roads, canals, and rails in the 1800s (map by National
Geographic Society)

incorporators received certain privileges that ranged from the right
to issue currency in the form of banknotes to monopoly franchises
[...] Members of corporations lost the freedom to write contracts
specifying their governance structures. Instead they had to accept
the form of organization imposed by the state. They also lost the
ability to add to their capital stock at will or to shift into new
lines of business as opportunities arose. In extreme cases, the laws
could be so restrictive as to limit opportunities for vertical inte-
gration. During the first four decades of the [nineteenth] century
only about one quarter of the corporations organized [in five states]

were manufacturing concerns [...] The vast majority of the corporations chartered [...] were either banks [...] or transportation companies.[6]

Albert Gallatin, in his report on the subject of public roads and canals, outlined proposals for what eventually became the Inland Waterway up the Atlantic coast, which was projected to include the Chesapeake and Delaware Canal, Susquehanna Canal and Dismal Swamp Canal, among other segments, together with roads and canals to the west, including an Ohio canal and Pittsburgh road. He anticipated that these would be federally financed, but in Jefferson's view this required a constitutional amendment, which was sought but not forthcoming. As observed by Henry Adams:

> Supposing the Administration to be pledged to the policy outlined by Gallatin and approved by Jefferson in the Annual Message of 1806, the New York commissioners applied to Congress for assistance and uniting with other local interests procured the passage of Calhoun's bill for internal improvements. They were met by Madison's veto [in 1817]. This act, although at first it seemed to affect most the interests of New York, was in reality injurious only to the Southern states. Had the government lent its aid to the Erie Canal it must have assisted similar schemes elsewhere. The Middle states were far in advance of the Eastern and Southern in opening communication with the West.[7]

Madison's veto message declared:

> it does not appear that the power purported to be exercised by the bill is among the enumerated powers or that it falls by any just interpretation within the power to make laws necessary and proper [...] I am not unaware of the great importance of roads and canals and the improved navigation of water courses, and that a power in the National Legislature to provide for them might be exercised with signal advantage to the general prosperity [...] [I]ts beneficial objects might be attained by a resort for the necessary powers to the same

wisdom and virtue in the nation which established the Constitution in its actual form and providently marked out in the instrument itself a safe and practicable mode of improving it as experience may suggest.[8]

President Monroe unsuccessfully sought a constitutional amendment.[9] In the next three decades, Gallatin's design was largely carried out by state and local governments. Gallatin's design was that:

> the United States may with the assent of the states undertake some of the works at their sole expense or they may subscribe a certain number of shares of the stock of companies incorporated for that purpose. Loans might also in some instances be made to such companies […] details would probably be executed on a more economical plan by private companies.[10]

With respect to the Cumberland road then under way using federal funds with the assent of the state, Gallatin suggested that it be financed "either by loans or becoming shareholders and the last mode appears the most eligible."[11] It has been said that:

> Attempts to revive the authority of a central government by controlling the distribution of public land, empowering a central bank, raising the tariff, and funding a network of interior transportation— sometimes called the American System—called the roll of policies that the enemies of hierarchy would topple in the 1830s and 1840s.[12]

Of this design, Henry Adams said:

> Naturally the improvements thus contemplated were so laid out as to combine and satisfy local interests. The advantage which Mr. Gallatin proposed to gain was that of combining these interests in advance, so that they should cooperate in one great system instead of wasting the public resources in isolated efforts. He wished to fix the policy of government for at least ten years, and probably for an indefinite time, on the whole subject of internal improvements, as he had already succeeded in fixing it in regard to the payment of debt. By thus establishing a complete national system to be executed by

degrees, the whole business of annual chaffering and log-rolling for local appropriations in Congress, and all its consequent corruptions and inconsistencies were to be avoided.[13]

Further,

> a system of internal improvement should be created commensurate with the magnitude of the country; "by these operations new channels of communication will be opened between the states, the lines of separation will disappear, their interests will be identified, and then united by new and indissoluble ties."[14]

In the words of a later historian:

> He wanted to see all expenditures reduced and some completely abolished until the debt had been repaid. That came first. Having accomplished that, he would have sanctioned government expenditures on internal improvements to the extent of the revenue, for this was the only legitimate, non-capital-destroying form of government spending so far as he was concerned.[15]

In his last message to Congress in November 1808, just after Gallatin's report, President Jefferson declared:

> Redemption [of the national debt] once effected [...] the revenue thereby liberated may, by a just repartition among the states and a correspondent amendment of the Constitution, be applied, in time of peace, to rivers, canals, roads, arts, manufactures and other great objects within each state.

Henry Adams made the jaundiced comment that:

> John Randolph might wonder to see him stride so fast and far toward what had been ever denounced as Roman imperialism and corruption [...] putting into the hands of the central government an instrument of corruption and making the states stipendiaries of Congress.
> [...]

> He no longer talked of "a wise and frugal government which
> shall restrain men from injuring one another, which shall leave
> them otherwise free to regulate their own pursuits of industry and
> improvement and shall not take from the mouth of labour the bread
> it has earned."[16]

Adams described the scheme calling for $2 million per year for
ten years as "so extensive in its scope that no European monarch
except perhaps the Czar could have equalled its scale."[17]

Contrary to the views of those who contend that the American
Constitution was a charter of the property rights of private corporations, the American-chartered private business corporation was
almost unknown at the time of its framing. In his classic study
of the earlier history of American corporations, John Stancliffe
Davis demonstrated that only a handful of corporate charters were
granted during the colonial period of American history. By 1700,
there were five surviving municipal charters.[18] In the eighteenth
century, there were more, but only 16 or 17 survived until the
Revolution.[19] There were ecclesiastical and charitable private corporations, including nine colleges by the time of the Revolution.[20]
But "business corporations [...] were few, and on the whole of no
great importance. Only as the colonial period drew to a close did
several come into existence, and even these were hardly typical of
present-day business corporations."[21] There were libraries and a
handful of insurance companies and banks. "No 'general incorporation act' permitting 'freedom of incorporation' in accordance with its provisions was known in America in the colonial
days."[22] The first such act, for aqueduct companies, was enacted in
Massachusetts in 1799.[23]

The first corporation to be chartered to build transportation arteries was one for the Susquehanna Canal incorporated in
1783. A total of 74 canal charters were issued by 1800.[24] In 1785,
Maryland and Virginia together bought one-fifth of the stock in
a corporation to improve navigation on the Potomac River.[25] By
the time work was finished the two states had furnished more than
half the capital by buying shares.[26] Virginia bought shares in projects for improvement to the James River, the Shenandoah, and
a Dismal Swamp Canal; the City of Norfolk also bought shares.

New York bought shares in a Western Canal company. There was a wide variety of toll-supported canal projects in which state governments bought stock in the period before 1801, none of which were notably successful. As to canals, "the corporate form proved unequal to the task."[27]

There were 73 eighteenth-century toll bridge corporations,[28] as well as 72 turnpike companies.[29] Most of these functioned without state or local investments.

In a letter to Gallatin reprinted with his report, Robert Fulton, the inventor of the steamship, declared of Gallatin's vision:

> it is necessary to bind the states together by the people's interests one of which is to enable every man to sell the produce of his labour at the best market and purchase at the cheapest. This accords with the idea of Hume that the government of a wise people would be little more than a system of civil police for the best interest of man is industry and a free exchange of the produce of his labour for the things which he may require.[30]

In this way, what later became the Whig American system of public improvements was reconciled with Jeffersonian ideals of limited government.

Of Gallatin's grand design, Henry Adams, usually a critic of the Jeffersonians, was to observe:

> to make a comprehensive permanent provision for the moral and economical development of the people, to mark out the path of progress with precision and to enter upon it at least so far as to make subsequent advances easy and certain, this was the highest statesmanship, the broadest practical philanthropy.[31]

In the pre-Civil War American economy,

> the elected public official replaced the individual enterpriser as the key figure in the release of capitalist energy; the public treasury rather than private capital became the major source of venture capital; and community purpose outweighed personal ambition in the selection

of large goals for local economies. "Mixed" enterprise was the customary organization for important innovations.[32]

Municipal incorporation as of right was provided for in most states on liberal terms, frequently long before the enactment of the general incorporation laws applicable to private corporations. As late as 1982, the minimum number of persons necessary to incorporate a municipality as of right was "75 in Alabama, 100 in Nebraska, New Mexico, Oregon and Wisconsin, 200 in Tennessee and 250 in Nevada."[33]

> The public function was viewed as an initial, developmental one. After enterprises became established on a profitable basis, city governments tended to transfer their investments to new projects and so, normally, a transition from public or quasi-public to private ownership and operation took place.[34]

The dimensions of mixed investment in Gallatin's program was considerable. After an initial investment in the National Road and federal acquisition of stock in the Chesapeake and Delaware Canal, the Chesapeake and Ohio Canal, the Dismal Swamp Canal, and a canal in Ohio, the federal government exited from the field except for aids to navigation and military roads in the West. In 1812, because of impending war, Secretary Gallatin announced that the federal cupboard was bare. President Madison vetoed federal appropriations contained in a Bonus Bill in 1817 on constitutional grounds. President Monroe vetoed a proposed investment in toll roads in 1822, though he signed proposed aid for the Chesapeake and Delaware Canal on his last day in office. On May 27, 1830, President Jackson delivered his memorable veto message of the Maysville Road bill, alluding to "losses of unsuccessful private speculation," "unconstitutional expenditures for the purchase of corrupt influence," and a desire to keep business out of government, while expressing the view that public funds would be "more judiciously applied and economically expended under the direction of the state legislatures."[35] Because the revenue source for proposed internal improvements was the protective tariff, appropriation bills for them were opposed by most Southerners, though not by Clay and Calhoun. In 1840, Governor Seward of New York, though urging revenue bond issues, observed that "taxation for internal improvement deservedly finds no advocate."[36] In 1842 and 1846, New York barred loans to private corporations and provided for bond referenda. Similar bans were enacted by Wisconsin in 1848 and Michigan in 1850. New York, Maryland, Pennsylvania, and Virginia loaned or invested large sums in canals and railroads. With the exception of the Erie Canal, most of the canal investments were non-productive, leading to defaults by Maryland and Pennsylvania, among other states. In Pennsylvania, nine counties and ten municipalities took up the slack. In 1857, a reaction against defaults resulted in a ban on state aid to private corporations and on stock subscriptions by local governments, approved in a referendum by a majority of nine to one. In 1857, Pennsylvania sold a portion of its interest in the Pennsylvania main railroad line to the Pennsylvania Railroad at a considerable loss; the state continued to hold more than half the stock. Maryland sold its stock in the Baltimore and Ohio Railroad in 1867; the City of Baltimore, which broke even on its investment apart from the economic development benefits, did not sell its shares until 1890. By 1860, $400 million had been invested in internal improvements by governments, about $300 million by states (including $70 million by New York and $50 million by Virginia) and $125 million by about 100 local governments.

After the Civil War, various states made $60 million to $70 million in railroad investments. Reconstruction legislatures in the South were alleged to have been especially profligate. Eight Southern states defaulted during reconstruction; there were local defaults in 25 states.[37]

In the pre-Civil War era, roughly 70 percent of the investment in canals and 25–30 percent of that in railroads was from governments. In the period 1861–73, about 15 percent of the investment in railroads was governmental, including very large land grants. After 1873, public investments in railroads were negligible.

After the Civil War, the federal government made a cash investment in the Union Pacific Railway; it owned stock and had directors on its board until 1897. It was said by Goodrich that "in any other country [...] [it] would have been built by the government as a military road." He adds, "Small groups of investors venturing very little capital of their own were able to build the roads with the money of the bondholders and the government and to pay themselves quick and extraordinary returns."[38] Virginia's pre-Civil War railroad and canal investments took the form of stock ownership so as not to "obtrude upon the detailed administration."[39]

The private railroad or banking corporation with publicly appointed directors and, later, the public development corporation with private directors have been familiar political phenomena throughout American history. As Lively points out:

> As an early American institution [...] the corporation was a public school for enterprise. Its graduates were never very loyal, but they were no less obligated to it for their experience with major engineering projects, their knowledge of managerial problems, and their skill at gathering and handling large capital.
>
> [...]
>
> [N]o one has undertaken extended or precise description of the way public and private obligations were combined by officers and public guardians of ante-bellum mixed corporations [who] defined the character of business-government relationships, the duty of corporation to public, and the responsibility of manager to investor. Customary procedures and standards of behaviour for managers of the modern corporation were thus conceived in ideological twilight, and had become habitual before the individual entrepreneur achieved a firm grip on the corporate form. Perhaps from the divided loyalties of the public-spirited men who planned so boldly for early community growth there emerged the ethical confusion characteristic of subsequent corporate behaviour.[40]

There was an explosion of municipal debt and enterprise in two periods: in the 1840s after several states which had engaged in private loans and investments (Arkansas, Florida, Louisiana, Illinois, Indiana, Maryland, Michigan, Mississippi, and Pennsylvania) defaulted on their bonds, with local debt increasing from $25 million in 1840 to $200 million in 1860; and again in the 1870s and 1880s after redeemer governments in Southern states clamped down on state debt issues, prompting a further increase in local debt to $821 million in 1880. Cities resorted to revenue and special-assessment bonds to avoid or overcome state-imposed limits on local government debt. In addition,

> another method of circumventing debt limits was to create new forms of local government, special districts such as school, park or water districts that had their own authority to borrow or levy taxes. This was a way of making the same property do double, triple or even more duty in financing local governmental investment and service provision.[41]

So-called "shadow governments," alleged to have a trillion dollars in debt, are thus of increasing concern in today's America.[42]

It remains true that "intergovernmental competition in a federal system may have been one of the key elements of American development through space and time."[43] In the early to mid nineteenth century, as stated by Eric Monkkonen:

> municipal corporations were the dominant type of corporations [...] the difficulties of obtaining private corporation charters prior to the general incorporation statutes [...] made municipalities the best outlets for the savings of strangers [...] Municipalities competed fiercely with one another for development.[44]

Many of the early public–private organizations were business corporations in which governments took shares and seats on the board; others were municipalities exercising proprietary functions but few governmental ones. These entities, organized on well-established and generally understood principles and subject to clear rules, were far more successful than today's purpose-built "community development corporations," which have been said to be:

> good for the psyches of boards of directors of foundations [...] but the multiplier effect is small and their contagion is yet to be proven, [they are] far more complex in their organization and finances than conventional developments in either the public or private sectors.[45]

As observed by Charles Lindblom:

> the community organization movement has transformed the princi-
> pal burden of leadership into the hands of professionals. This is an
> extraordinary development, especially in a society that has so thor-
> oughly identified leadership in public affairs with the amateur or
> elected official.[46]

Gallatin's grand design was carried into execution by myriad state
and local governments. Responsibility had been unequivocally
allocated to them by the annual messages and veto messages of
Presidents Jefferson, Madison, Monroe, and Jackson. There is little in subsequent American history to suggest that a purely federal development would have been more successful, more honestly
administered, or less extravagant. The massive federal land grants
accompanying the construction of the transcontinental railroads
are not inspiring in this respect. The federal interstate highway
system, an accomplishment of the 1950s and 1960s, was an
impressive achievement, but it was seriously overbuilt, and the
massive migration to the suburbs that was its most important,
though unintended, effect might not have taken place if states and
localities and other vested interests such as railroads had more of
a voice in its design.

   Gallatin's report exemplified the appropriate federal role as
viewed by writers like Madison and Mill: the dissemination of
perspective and expertise, as distinct from the operation of programs. It was less prescriptive than the successful modern German
system of highly general federal "framework laws," but at least as
successful. America has seen nothing like it since; the last efforts
by the national government to even sketch national needs were
the Hoover Administration's study of *Recent Social Trends*[47] and
the early and aborted work of the Roosevelt Administration's
National Resources Planning Board.[48] Fiscal stringency, whether
at the federal or state level, provides no excuse for not engaging in
constructive forethought. Many needed improvements and adap-
tations can be funded from user charges; a national study of the
potential of road-tolling and time-of-day pricing of roads would
be of great value. The same applies to the potential use of the

internet in education, and the chance it offers for adjusting down-ward the age and grade level that demarcates the responsibilities of our generally successful colleges and our failing high schools, as in Quebec, where the twelfth grade is the start of college rather than the end of high school. It is doubtful that the high schools can be successfully reformed; they perhaps instead should be par-tially destroyed.

5

William Leggett and
the General Incorporation Laws

Today in the United States, we take for granted the right of individuals engaged in business to freely utilize the corporate form, with its advantages of limited personal liability, perpetual existence, and free transferability of shares. In most states, it requires only a few minutes, the presentation of one- or two-page Articles of Incorporation, and the payment of fees frequently amounting to only $50 or $100 to set up a corporation; the device is so standardized that for a very small company, the legal fees attending initial organization can amount to less than $1,000. In many other countries, there are elaborate educational requirements needed to incorporate businesses in certain fields, and elaborate investigations of the need for a business or its product.

In historical terms, general corporation laws are a rather recent development. After specially chartered corporations were involved in the "South Sea Bubble" investment scandals in the eighteenth century, the British Parliament passed the "Bubble Act" in 1720 restraining special charters.[1] The premise of the act was that the "Bubble" was due to incorporation rather than fraud, or that frauds were somehow facilitated by incorporation. Under the pressure of increasingly liberal economic opinion, the "Bubble Act" was repealed, and in 1844 a Companies Registration Act allowing free incorporation was enacted in Britain.

11. William Leggett, assistant editor of *The Evening Post*, 1829–36 (The Miriam and Ira D. Wallach Division of Art, Prints and Photographs: Print Collection, The New York Public Library (1900–10))

The new act obviated the need to have resort to limited partnerships, business trusts, or joint stock companies to evade the Bubble Act and secure the benefit of limited liability. As early as 1811, New York allowed free incorporation in certain classes of industry, with the proviso that the resulting corporations could only endure for 20 years and have a capital of $100,000. Although progressives in the twentieth century were to question free incorporation, it was favored by their counterparts during the Jackson period, and the general incorporation laws were regarded as attacks on special privilege by Jacksonian reformers like Theodore Sedgwick, William Gouge, and John Vethake; they were described as "partly an expression of the longing for equality."[2] Special laws were reproached because they frequently conferred monopolies, were accompanied by exemptions from jury and militia service,

12. A painting of William Leggett by Erastus Salisbury Field (1805–1900)
from 1835 (Public domain)

were joined with tax exemptions, included the right of eminent
domain, or authorized the issuance of lotteries. At the time, special
acts for turnpike companies, railroads, canals, and street improvements were becoming increasingly common. There were said to be
about 2,000 corporations chartered by special act in New England
by 1830; by 1861, a dozen states had actually forbidden incorporation by special act in their constitutions.

William Leggett, a leading dramatist and newspaper writer,
was the most vociferous champion of general incorporation laws,
in reaction to the Panic of 1837. A colorful figure, he was born in
1801, and, after working as a lumberjack and spending a year
in college at Georgetown, he enlisted in the Navy; he was court-
martialed at an early age, his sentence being reduced to time served
prior to trial. He subsequently became a poet, short-story writer,
and dramatist, before finding his true vocation as a turbulent
newspaper writer in self-published journals and in the *New York*

Evening Post, from which he was separated after antagonizing all of its public agency advertisers. In this period, he engaged in a duel with a man named Blake. On being asked why he chose a lame poet as a second, he declared "Blake's second, Berkeley, was lame, and I did not propose that the d----d Englishman should beat me at anything."[3] He was the author of several books of short stories: *Leisure Hours at Sea* (1825), *Tales and Sketches of a Country Schoolmaster* (1835), and *Naval Stories* (1835). He served as theater critic for the *New York Mirror* and assistant editor of the *Merchants Telegraph*. In 1838, he briefly self-published a literary journal, *The Critic*, which folded after six months. In the summer of 1829, he went to work for William Cullen Bryant's *New York Evening Post*, becoming an owner and editor in 1831. In 1834–5, he served as editor while Bryant was away in Europe, and so antagonized the newspaper's advertisers that he was obliged to leave; he then started his own small newspapers, the *Plaindealer* (1836) and the *Examiner* (1837). Bryant later wrote of him: "What he would not yield to the dictates of interest he was still less disposed to yield to the suggestions of fear."[4] He was a founder of and unsuccessful congressional candidate for the short-lived but influential Equal Rights or Loco-Foco Party in New York City.[5] The Loco-Foco Party arose from "the meeting at Tammany Hall in 1835, when the Conservative or 'bank' Democrats turned off the lights, whereupon the 'Equal Rights' faction lit the newly introduced loco-foco matches and took possession of the hall."[6]

As described by Jeffrey Sklansky:[7]

> in the winter of 1836–1837, Leggett applied the same principle to
> merchants' associations as to trade unions. Business combination
> in itself posed nothing to fear, he argued, for as soon as merchants
> colluded to engross flour or any other necessity, they invited com-
> petition that would restore prices to their "natural value." "[B]oth
> the principles of free trade, and the plainest principles of natural
> equity require, that men should be left at liberty to pursue by con-
> cert, if they choose, any object they have a right to achieve by indi-
> vidual action. The safety of the community against extortionate and
> intolerant combinations is sufficiently insured by the effect of com-
> petition and the influence of publick opinion," he wrote, showing a

faith notably absent from his lament over the "passion and caprice" of newspaper readers. The real cause of exorbitant prices, according to Leggett, lay not in the market but in the legislature, whose special charters for banks were sustaining the inflationary bubble. And the cure was to be found not by opposing business combination, but by demanding that it be made equally accessible to working people through a general incorporation law, which would turn incorporation into a basic right of all qualified applicants instead of a special privilege conferred by the legislature. [...] "Combination," he contended hopefully, was "an efficient weapon against the oppressor; but, like the sword bestowed by the good genius in the fairy tale, it shivers into fragments when drawn against the oppressed."[8]

His defense of the free market stemmed less from a commitment to individuals' freedom to pursue their calling, about which Leggett wrote only occasionally, than from a converse concern with the corruption of representative government through sponsorship of corporate monopolies, about which he wrote incessantly. He declared, however, that:

> The humblest citizens might associate together and wield through the agency of skilful and intelligent directors, chosen by themselves, a vast aggregate capital, composed of the little separate sums which they could afford to invest in such an enterprise, in competition with the capitals of the purse-proud men who now almost monopolize certain branches of business.[9]

Instead of channeling private wealth to serve public needs, he argued, the system of special charters made public servants into the agents of the irresponsible private entities they created. By delegating exclusive authority to favored groups of investors, the legislatures were "bartering away the sovereignty of the People to little bodies politic, fattening on the great body," conferring political power upon "a corporation; a body without a soul; an abstraction; a remote circumstance; nothing tangible or responsible." "The people of this great state fondly imagine that they govern themselves," he wrote, "but they do not! They are led about by the unseen but strong bands of chartered companies."[10]

In spearheading the successful drive for general incorporation laws, Leggett meant to limit the reach of market forces as much as to free them from unnatural constraints: popular sovereignty was properly priceless. In demanding the separation of business and state, as Marvin Meyers notes, Leggett sought to unhitch the market economy from speculative enterprise as much as to unfetter it from drags on its natural course. "We would withdraw all Government stimulants," he wrote, "[...] discontinuing the force-pump method, by which we now seek to make water flow up hill, and leaving it to flow in its own natural channels."[11] Zakim and Kornblith suggest that "The 'natural economy' he imagined was free-flowing yet confined to its proper place: 'an equal and uniform current, never stagnating, and never overflowing its boundaries,' like the limpid streams that gurgled through the pastoral landscapes of his western tales."[12] He considered that a general law would curb "those extremes of wealth and poverty so uniformly fatal to the liberties of mankind,"[13] and would in effect "incorporate the whole population of the State of New York, for every possible lawful purpose."[14]

Assuredly, he could be doctrinaire. He favored privatization of the postal service, notwithstanding constitutional authorization for it, regarding it as an extravagant menace: "to extend mail facilities into regions which perhaps God and nature meant should remain uninhabited for ages to come."[15] He feared "rapid and simultaneous diffusion of political intelligence, the obstruction of that of a contrary tenor, and the exercise of all the arts of political espionage—a dangerous institution."[16] He opposed municipal pensions for Revolutionary War veterans: "Have they [the City Council] any right under heaven to express their sympathy for the revolutionary pensioners at the city's cost?"[17] He was equally suspicious of endowed positions for university professors: "his interest is set as directly in opposition to his duty as it is possible to get."[18]

He was acclaimed by a twentieth-century North Dakota commentator as "one of the most sincere and brilliant apostles of democracy that America has ever known."[19] John Greenleaf Whittier wrote of Leggett that he "laboured more perseveringly and in the end more successfully [than any other man] to bring the practice of American democracy into conformity with its principles."[20] Upon his death, after Tammany Hall erected a bust of him in the room in which he had been expelled from the Democratic Party, Whittier wrote:

> Yes, pile the marble o'er him! It is well
> That ye who mocked him in his long stern strife
> And planted in the pathway of his life
> The ploughshares of your hatred hot from hell
>
> Who clamored down the bold reformer when
> He pleaded for his captive fellow-men
> Who spurned him in the market-place and sought
> Within thy walls, St. Tammany, to bind
> In party chains, the free and honest thought
> The angel utterance of an upright mind
>
> Well is it now that o'er his grave ye raise
> The stony tribute of your tardy praise
> For not alone that pile shall tell to fame
> Of the brave heart beneath, but of the builders' shame.[21]

Not to be outdone, William Cullen Bryant, a close associate of Leggett, similarly waxed poetical:

> The earth may ring, from shore to shore
> With echoes of a glorious name
> But he, whose loss and tears deplore
> Has left behind him more than fame
>
> For when the death-frost came to lie
> On Leggett's warm and mighty heart
> And quench his bold and friendly eye
> His spirit did not all depart
>
> His love of truth, too warm, too strong
> For Power or Fear to chain or chill

His hate of tyranny and wrong
Burn in the breasts he kindled still

The words of fire that from his pen
Were flung upon the fervid page
Still move still shake the hearts of men
Among a cold and coward age.[22]

Arthur Schlesinger for his part described Leggett as "the [Jacksonian] Democrat in whom social radicalism and anti-slavery united most impressively."[23] As White suggests: "Every extension of the sphere of government action beyond the Jeffersonian night-watchman duties, in his view, created a privileged aristocratic class at the expense of the productive laboring class."[24] His colleague Theodore Sedgwick Jr observed that "Every year was enlarging his character and widening the bounds of his liberality";[25] he had "softness and delicacy in his character which the acrimony of political strife had no effect to diminish."[26] Shortly before his death, he refused to trim for a nomination for Congress:

I have written my name in ineffaceable letters on the abolition record; and whether the reward ultimately comes in the shape of honors to the living man or a tribute to the memory of a departed one, I would not forfeit my right to it.[27]

Leggett died in 1839 after a short illness; his friends had hoped that he would recover from his illness in a warmer client and he had accordingly been appointed Minister to Guatemala by President Van Buren shortly before his death, though he never took up the post.

Leggett sought to foster "a system of legislation which leaves to all the free exercise of their talents and industry within the limits of the GENERAL LAW [...] the very measure to enable poor men to compete with the rich."[28] He favored universal suffrage and opposed registration requirements for voting. He opposed tariffs and state inspection laws. He did not favor recall of existing special charters, which would be allowed to expire by their own terms. Although the New York Equal Rights Party organized by Leggett, which seceded from the Democrats after his expulsion from Tammany Hall in 1835, never received more than 5,000 votes,[29]

> among their tangible accomplishments may be counted the New York State Free Banking Act of 1838 which repealed the Restraining Act of 1804 limiting note issuance to specially chartered banks,[30] the provision for a General Incorporation Law in the state's 1846 Constitution and, on the national level, the removal of federal government deposits from state banks by the Independent Treasury Act.[31]

The last statute was passed in 1840, was repealed by the Whigs in 1841, and was re-enacted in 1846. By 1850 there were 136 new banks, as against 73 special charter banks, giving "more capitalists access to and control over money supply [while] weakening systematic public control over their affairs."[32] Leggett took the view that "We must either have no chartered bank or we must have a national bank."

He sought a stable rather than speculative economy, and was a critic of "seasons of preternatural prosperity and severe distress, shaking public faith, exciting a spirit of wild speculation, demoralizing and vitiating the whole tone of popular sentiment and character."[33] He assailed "A gambling spirit [which] has infected the whole community—the offspring of our wretched undemocratic system of exclusive and partial legislation."[34] He favored free banking as well as free incorporation of corporations, but was willing to accept it only if banks' ability to issue small notes was curtailed: "It is the worst description of money and is generally bought [at a discount] to pay away to mechanics [...] Let employers provide themselves with gold to pay their hands."[35] "Free banking is the system pursued in Scotland, and that country escapes revulsions."[36]

Leggett was a consistent, but enlightened, champion of laissez-faire. He explicitly invoked the writings of Jeremy Bentham and Adam Smith, Thomas Jefferson and John Taylor. In a nativist period, he defended free immigration and also a "homesteading" approach to the disposal of public lands. Writing about supposed "foreign paupers," he observed:

> The earth is the heritage of man and these are a part of the heritors. We are not bound to support them; they must support themselves. If they are idle, let them starve; if they are vicious, let them be punished; but in God's name, as they bear God's image, let us not turn them away from a portion of that earth which was given by its Maker to all mankind, with no natural marks to designate the limits beyond which they may not freely pass. An influx of the hardy peasantry of Europe to fill up our waste lands and cover them with harvests is not a clog on our progress.[37]

With regard to public land, he claimed that:

> It would be no violation of the principles of free trade for the government which is the seller [...] to ask any price or make any conditions it thought proper in disposing of the publick lands [...] the greatest good of the greatest number—that mode of disposal which would lead to the largest amount of actual settlement upon and cultivation of the publick lands.[38]

The first American general incorporation law was that of Connecticut in 1837, followed by laws in New Jersey and Michigan in 1846 (all applicable to particular classes of business); that of New York in 1846 was the first true general incorporation law. (There had been a general law for the incorporation of religious organizations in New York as early as 1784.) Initially, these statutes imposed limits on maximum allowable capitalization; by 1920, virtually all these limits had been removed.[39] There were 341,000 incorporated companies in the United States in 1916, rising to 455,000 in 1926. In 1904, non-corporate entities like partnerships still produced a third of all manufactured goods; that percentage fell to 2.4 percent in 1920 as the corporate form carried all before it. By 1929, there were 1 million corporate shareholders, a number that increased to 12.5 million in 1959 and 31 million in 1970.

The ability to freely incorporate is basic to the American notion of free enterprise. Leggett assailed special charters that "limit the number of apprentices, fix the term of service, impose fines on all persons exercising their calling without becoming members of the corporation and exacting a heavy price for that privilege."[40] He similarly assailed occupational licensing laws that created "mere serfs and vassals, holding our dearest privileges [...] by the sufferance of our municipal servants."[41] The nineteenth-century reformer Park Godwin conceded that "Incorporations have conferred prodigious material benefits upon the nation," while asking "are they not masters of the nation?";[42] his predecessor William Cullen Bryant unambiguously believed that "their effect is good and wholesome."[43] There was rapid growth of corporate enterprise in the wake of the New York amendment before the Civil War.[44] In the words of E. Merrick Dodd,

> a system of factory production may live and grow under a system which holds the owners of an enterprise to full liability for its debts. But it will not grow so fast under that system as under one which makes industrial investment more attractive to the capitalist. If the average American of Jackson's or Polk's day liked to assert his equality with his neighbor, he liked even better to improve his financial status by quicker methods than engaging in productive labor.[45]

The legal historian James Willard Hurst for his part observed that "by legitimating and supporting broad freedom of private association for purposes of education, religion, welfare and business, law made its main contribution to adjustment of social context by other than legal processes."[46]

> The function of corporation law was to enable businessmen to act, not to police their action [...] For both small and large enterprises, the corporation provided a defined, legally protected and practically firm position of authority for those in central control [...] The corporate form distinctively helped muster capital for small firms by providing a standard format within which to combine investors active in management with investors who desired a more passive role. The corporation helped muster capital for the large firm by

legitimating a flexible structure of shares and long-term debt, protecting management's discretion in retaining earnings and providing assured limited liability for stockholders.[47]

The last function became important only with the rise of investment banking in the 1890s. By 1900, corporations produced two-thirds of US manufacturing output, a figure that reached 95 percent in the 1960s.[48]

Later amendments to the general incorporation laws gave them even greater flexibility by allowing companies to opt out of various standard provisions.[49] To again quote Hurst: "there was an emerging demand for a convenient business association with affairs of limited import on the community, far removed from high politics." While the progressives of a later time on occasion sought to limit use of the corporate form either by prohibiting the corporate practice of professions[50] or by seeking to impose size limits,[51] their essential strategy has involved either use of regulatory agencies or application of the antitrust law, and the wisdom of general incorporation statutes is no longer much debated. Creditors are left to protect themselves through contract, credit reporting, and insolvency remedies; as Hurst put it: "we ceased to build general social controls into corporate structure because the large business corporation grew to involve a wider range of interests than the corporation's own internal constitution could mediate."[52]

Ease of incorporation and consequent freedom of establishment is a little-appreciated but essential feature of the American economy. Leggett's intervention was decisive in the popularization and proliferation of the concept. In our time, new forms of business structure have been made available to citizens as of right: limited liability corporations and partnerships; S corporations; so-called B corporations for profit-making entities authorized in 12 states in order to free corporations from the rule of *Dodge v. Ford*[53] making shareholder interests paramount over those of labor, the environment, and other constituencies; residential community associations, condominiums, and time-shares. There is almost certainly scope for adjustment of our zoning laws to make Planned Unit Developments available as of right to developers; there may also be scope for allowing citizens at sub-municipal levels to organize block-level land readjustment associations, cooperative old age clubs, and perhaps even election-precinct-level associations like the British parish councils with limited taxing powers. The use for public purposes of small voluntary associations is founded on the recognition that "because the members of a voluntary community already share common interests, consensus can be achieved more easily." In addition, such organizations do not suffer from a vice of large polities, where "the concentrated resources of minorities will tend to overwhelm and overtax the resources of unorganized majorities."[54]

6

Justin Morrill and
Land Grant Colleges

The process of establishing state universities was well advanced by 1862, and a number of universities and private colleges had received ad hoc land grants from state governments, including William and Mary College (20,000 acres), Harvard College (3,300 acres), Dartmouth College (40,960 acres), and Dickinson College, Franklin College, and Reading Academy (5,000 acres each). By 1805 there were state universities in Georgia, North Carolina, South Carolina, and Tennessee. In 1816, Virginia had established its Central College, converted by Jefferson into the most famous of state universities. Proposals for a national university made by President Washington in his message to Congress in 1790, by Jefferson in a message to Congress in 1806, and by Joel Barlow in 1806 were stillborn because of constitutional objections; similar proposals by Charles Fleischmann in 1838 to use the Smithson endowment for a national agricultural college and by Land Office Commissioner John Wilson in 1853 for a university in the District of Columbia also failed.

It is possible to take the view that the groundwork for the Morrill Act was laid not by Senator Justin Morrill of Vermont but by the great mental health reformer Dorothea Dix. In 1848, she memorialized Congress to grant 5 million acres of land to be divided among the states and sold by them to build facilities for care of the insane. A variant of the proposal passed the House in 1852 and in 1854 Congress approved another version of the bill,

13. Hon. Justin Smith Morrill of Vermont (Library of Congress)

which was vetoed by President Pierce on constitutional grounds. There was a minor precedent for the proposed grant in the form of a federal grant of land in 1826 to a deaf and dumb asylum in Kentucky.

In 1852, Congressman Henry Bennett of New York proposed a similar system of land grants to Western states for railroads and to the non-public land states for common schools. This bill passed the House but ultimately failed in 1855.

A proposal for agricultural colleges had been made by Jonathan Baldwin Turner of Illinois in 1851 and had united agricultural reformers in the coastal states and in the public land states. The original measure proposed a grant of 20,000 acres for each senator or representative in Congress, with scrip exchangeable for Western land instead of land being issued to the Eastern coastal states; the scrip was intended to be sold to third parties to prevent one state

14. Senator Justin Smith Morrill House, Strafford, Orange County, VT
(Library of Congress)

from owning land in another. The act passed the Congress but was vetoed by President Buchanan.[1] It had been lauded by Stephen Douglas, who regarded himself as a latter-day Jeffersonian, as "the most democratic scheme of education ever proposed to the mind of man."[2]

Justin Morrill was born in 1810. He attended academies in Thetford and Randolph, Vermont, but never went to college. He worked in mercantile establishments in Strafford, Vermont, and Portland, Maine until he was 38; he was successful enough to retire to life as a gentleman farmer. He designed and constructed an 18-room neo-Gothic wooden house, and accompanying gardens, in Strafford; it is now a tourist attraction.

He was a delegate to the Whig convention that nominated General Winfield Scott for president in 1852, and was elected to the House of Representatives in 1855 as a Whig, becoming a Republican two years later; in 1867, he was elected to the US Senate, where he served until his death 31 years later. He opposed the spread of slavery, but was willing to tolerate it where it existed: "from the clearest light we have from above, from history, from experience, from the combined testimony of good men of all ages, slavery is wrong."[3]

As a congressman, he successfully sponsored the Lincoln Administration's protectionist Tariff Act of 1861, sometimes compared by some in the South to the 1828 Tariff of Abominations. Enactment of the bill was made possible by the secession of Southern congressmen. During the Civil War, he sponsored two additional tariff bills aimed at raising revenues, which raised rates further. He also sponsored the Anti-Bigamy Act of 1862, aimed at practices of the Mormon Church, regarding these as "gross offenses whether in secular or ecclesiastical garb; to prevent practices which outrage the moral sense of the Christian world."[4] Vermonters of the period disliked Brigham Young and Joseph Smith, both of whom had their origins there. The act was effectively a dead letter until the Mormons renounced polygamy in 1890, an incident of Utah's efforts to gain statehood.

In sponsoring the famous statute that bears his name, he declared:

> This bill proposes to establish at least one college in every state upon a sure and perpetual foundation, accessible to all, where all of needful science for the practical avocations of life shall be taught, where neither the higher graces of classical studies nor that military drill that our country now so greatly appreciates will be entirely ignored, and where agriculture, the foundation of all present and future prosperity, may look for troops of earnest friends, studying its familiar and recondite economics, and at last elevating it to that higher level where it may fearlessly invoke comparison with the most advanced standards of the world.

Morrill had become interested in agricultural education in consequence of sharply falling crop yields resulting from exhaustion of soils. Wheat and potato production in New England fell by almost half between 1840 and 1850; there was also a sharp fall in tobacco production in Virginia. In 1856, Morrill had unsuccessfully sponsored legislation to create a national agriculture college modeled on the military academies. He was impressed by the existence of agricultural colleges abroad, such as in England and especially in France, which had five agricultural colleges and about 100 less formal agricultural schools.[5]

After the Civil War, he became a member of the influential Committee of Fifteen on Reconstruction. In the 1890s, in the run-up to the Spanish–American War, he was a strong anti-imperialist: he opposed President Grant's proposed annexation of Santo Domingo as well as the annexation of Hawaii and Puerto Rico. As for American designs on Mexico, he declared that Mexico had "more of the Latin race than the stomach of Uncle Sam can safely bear."[6] On the other hand, he thought that Canada would ultimately be absorbed by the United States. He was awarded an honorary doctorate by Johns Hopkins in 1887. The later stages of his Senate career were informed by three main interests: tariffs, sound money, and the architecture of the US Capitol and its vicinity. He favored tariffs for both protection and revenue, and played a leading role not only in Civil War tariff increases but in the McKinley Tariff of 1890, the Wilson–Gorman Tariff legislation of 1894 and the Dingley Tariff of 1897. His high-tariff legacy, beneficial to the North and Midwest and ruinous to the South, lasted until the advent of the Wilson Administration in 1913. In general, he favored fixed rather than *ad valorem* tariffs, since the latter were less effective as protectionist devices during recessions when they were most needed. Consistent with his views, he also opposed reciprocal trade agreements, including one with Canada, regarding free trade as "a sunlit theory, rejected by every civilized nation." He opposed the use of greenbacks as legal tender during the Civil War: "I protest against making anything legal tender but gold and silver as calculated to undermine all confidence in [the] Republic."[7] He also opposed bi-metallism, and in 1875 was successful in limiting the amount of greenback circulation to $300 million; in 1863 he had similarly compromised, declaring that "the patient has got accustomed to opiates and the dose cannot be withheld without peril." It was said that "probably his greatest contribution in the Senate was his attempt to restore a sound currency."[8] In his last years in the Senate, prior to his death in 1898, he arranged for construction of what is now the main (Jefferson) building of the Library of Congress and of improvements to the Capitol and its grounds.

In 1862, a revised act providing 30,000 acres for each member of Congress was signed by President Lincoln. The act contemplated sale of the lands and scrip by the states, and the reinvestment of the proceeds at 5 percent interest. Two states, Illinois and New York, evaded the feature of the act relating to scrip. The state university in Illinois entered 26,000 acres in Minnesota and years later reaped a good return; California realized more than $5.00 per acre and Minnesota $4.39, according to Allan Nevins.[9] New York conveyed its scrip to Ezra Cornell, who used it to acquire a half-million acres in Wisconsin, which were actively managed for many years and ultimately yielded the university $5,765,000, as compared with $300,000 realized by Wisconsin's agricultural college from the sale of scrip. The single largest allocation was to the New York State Agricultural College at Cornell. In addition to provision for the Northern states, five public land states which had seceded were to receive scrip for 900,000 acres when they re-entered the Union, and Texas, which had much public land of its own, received scrip for 180,000 acres, netting it $156,000. This delay benefited the five states; Arkansas and Florida got 90 cents per acre for their scrip when sold in 1872 and 1873; the Eastern states got from 40 to 60 cents per acre on their earlier sales. After 1870, the value of unredeemed college scrip rose to $1.00 or more per acre. The total grant was of 17 million acres; the liquidation of the grants by state governments were resented in the public land states by reason of their depressing effect on the land market. After reconstruction, the Morrill Act was extended to 16 Southern states. In total, 48 agricultural colleges were created or expanded to secure the benefits of the act, including some African-American institutions in four Southern states. New institutions were created in Oklahoma, Indiana (Purdue), New York (Cornell), Texas, and Washington; among existing institutions creating new programs were Brown, Dartmouth, Yale, Rutgers, and MIT. The original act included a provision for the teaching of military tactics by the new colleges, inspired by early Northern defeats in the Civil War, in addition to the provisions for training in agricultural (including forestry, veterinary medicine, and home economics) and mechanical (engineering) arts. The contemplated training was to be "without excluding other scientific and classical studies."[10] The military training provision, which in the early years consisted of little besides drilling, was greatly expanded by the National Defense Act of 1916, which gave rise to the Reserve Officers' Training Corps system that had trained 50,000 officers by World War II, three-fourths of all active military officers; half of the reserve officers were trained in the land grant colleges. The land grant colleges are credited with fundamentally altering the pre-existing class basis of American higher education.[11]

The land grant colleges had a profound effect on high schools, which were virtually nonexistent outside the North-east; many of them could only obtain a student body by giving preparatory courses to entering students. The availability of college training to students of limited means stimulated the creation of high schools, the colleges functioning as accrediting agencies in many states. Morrill's purpose was:

> to largely benefit those at the bottom of the ladder who want to climb up, or those who have some ambition to rise in the world, but are without the means to seek far from home a higher standard of culture. This and more was sought to be accomplished by bringing forward at less cost of time and money, courses of study, [...] of greater use in practical affairs than those then largely prevailing, which seemed to offer little of lasting value beyond mere discipline imposed.[12]

The beginnings of the land grant colleges were humble. Daniel J. Boorstin has observed that among the 48 recipients of grants were new state colleges and universities in 11 states, eight new "agricultural and mechanical" (A&M) colleges, and six colleges for African-Americans.[13] Virtually none of the students at the African-American colleges did college work; it was not until 1930 that college students at those institutions exceeded the students in preparatory programs. The influence of the act caused the number of non-military engineering schools to increase from four in 1860 to 70 in 1872. By 1976, about 40 percent of all engineering degrees were granted by land grant colleges.[14] A conference of the new institutions took place in 1871 at which Daniel Coit Gilman of Yale, later president of Johns Hopkins, lamented the state of public schools: "we have hardly anything to prepare for the scientific schools," a situation that continues to obtain. In 1867, Gilman had described the land grant colleges as, potentially, "national schools of science."[15]

There were further conferences in 1872, 1881, 1883, and 1885; in 1887 an association of land grant colleges was formed which thereafter held annual meetings. In 1882, after 20 years, total land grant enrolment was only 2,243 but it rose to 25,000 in 1895; 135,000, one-third of the students in higher education, by 1916; and 400,000 by 1926. By 1910, according to Boorstin, only one-third of the financial support of land grant colleges came from the federal government and that proportion had dropped to one-tenth by 1932. In 1935, additional federal funds of $17.5 million per year for instruction, research, and extension work, mostly the latter, were provided by the Bankhead–Jones Act. In 1887, Congress, by enacting the Hatch Act, gave each state a $15,000 annual grant for the creation of agricultural experiment stations, usually attached to the A&M colleges; from them came the soybean industry, hybrid corn, and streptomycin. In 1906, Congress passed the Adams Act, according each experiment station an additional, phased-in $15,000 per year, but requiring them to submit proposed projects to the Department of Agriculture. The Purnell Act in 1925 provided an additional $60,000 for each station. Many colleges established engineering experiment stations with state funds, but the appropriations for these never exceeded about one-tenth of what was spent on the agricultural stations. The Smith–Lever Act in 1914 provided for dissemination of agricultural research through a federally funded extension service attached to each agricultural college; each state received $10,000 plus an additional appropriation to be matched by the state based on its rural population. By 1919, 75 percent of the nation's counties had county extension agents and 35 percent had home demonstration agents who visited farms.[16] By 1951, total federal appropriations amounted to $5 million for instruction, $12.5 million for experiment stations, and $32 million for extension work. In 1966, a Current Research Information System for agricultural research was established that may be a model for other disciplines.

After the withdrawal of the Southern states from Congress, it was no longer seen as necessary to use land grants rather than cash appropriations to avoid constitutional constraints. Nonetheless, there were further abortive proposals for aid to women's colleges and for public schools in the District of Columbia, which had been excluded from the Morrill Act. In 1872 and 1873, measures to grant lands to agricultural colleges passed one house, and another measure passed the Senate in 1872. Finally, in 1890, the Second Morrill Act was passed after a lapse of 28 years, granting $15,000 for each state and territory for its land grant institutions each year, rising by $1,000 per year to $25,000. These sums seem modest, but they exceeded the sums spent by land grant institutions on agricultural education in 1890 and were greater than the income the institutions received from the endowments provided from the sale of the lands granted in 1862. The 1890 act denied funds to colleges "where a distinction of race or color is made in the admission of students," but allowed grants to predominantly African-American institutions. The institutions that became South Carolina State University and Kentucky State University became land grant institutions in 1896 and 1897; 11 African-American land grant institutions were created in all as a result of a requirement in the Second Morrill Act that the states fairly divide funds between black and white institutions, with annual reports to Congress. In 1968 the District of Columbia, with a grant of $7.24 million, and in 1994 29 Native American tribal colleges were added to the system.

The act was significant in that it did not provide for micro-management but looked toward the creation under state auspices and the permanent endowment of new types of institutions. It required participating states to formally accept its terms within two years, required annual reports, and required return of granted funds if a college was not in operation within five years, but otherwise did not constrain the states. Income from the original grant of 17 million acres amounted in 1953 to only about $1,750,000, but the act was a vital catalyst when it was enacted, even though most of the states received only enough annual income to pay two or three professors, and received no capital funds. In spite of its modesty, the subsequent structure of experiment stations and extension services led Samuel Eliot Morison and Henry Steele Commager to call it "the most important piece of agricultural legislation in American history."[17] The existing state universities, whose creation had been stimulated by the reservation of two townships in each state provided for by admission laws following the Northwest Ordinance, began to themselves offer agricultural and engineering programs, and the A&M colleges for their part offered liberal arts programs. By 1963, the convergence was so complete that the Office of Education ceased maintaining separate statistics on the land grant institutions.

By the beginning of World War II, state university systems had grown, but had not reached their present importance. Their total enrolment was roughly equal to that in private colleges, many of them of denominational origin. The impetus to the postwar explosion of public higher education was found in the GI Bill of Rights and subsequent federal scholarship and loan programs. Private institutions were more conservative than their public counterparts in grasping the opportunity for growth presented by the new legislation; whether from civic apathy or the reduced vitality of religious denominations, few new private institutions were founded after World War II (Brandeis University is probably the most noted one), although more recently there have been new institutions inspired by religious fundamentalism (Liberty University, Regent University, Patrick Henry College, Bob Jones University, Oral Roberts University, and the Catholic Ave Maria University). State governments have proliferated new campuses, and some of their efforts have been impressive: for example, the state university system in New York and the North Carolina community college system. Typically, the new institutions in the public sector have been currently funded rather than endowed. Some of the developments under state charter school laws have promise; however, in all but a few states (Arizona and Louisiana being the exceptions), little has been done to bring them up to scale; one may contrast the recent British legislation providing for creation of secondary school academies, some enjoying private sector or sectarian assistance, which already account for

2,456 British secondary schools.[18] There also has been little effort, in either the public or private sector, to create schools for the gifted and talented, like the recently revived Speyer School in the New York City public school system, or specialized language and science high schools, all of which could usefully be initially endowed by federal or state governments. Instead, all energies and funds are devoted to the feeding of, and futile efforts to reform, the present system.

The GI Bill of Rights, enacted in 1944, has received astonishingly little attention from American historians, law professors, and political scientists. In the 60 years since its enactment, only two books about it have been published, one a short monograph issued by the University Press of Kentucky and the other a book by a retired journalist issued by a small commercial publisher. Had the bill been a product of the Roosevelt or Kennedy Administrations, America's lemming-like academics would be falling over themselves acclaiming its wisdom. The difficulty is that the bill in its entirety was prepared by obscure officers of the American Legion; its principal Senate sponsor was Senator Bennett Champ Clark of Missouri, known for his alcoholic propensities, and its House manager until just before its enactment was Congressman John Rankin of Mississippi, second only to Senator Theodore Bilbo as Congress's most notorious racist. Both, however, were exceptionally able parliamentarians.

The Roosevelt Administration's planning for veterans had been affected by the president's previous record of opposition to bonus proposals put forth on behalf of World War I veterans and his rhetoric favoring universal and not veteran-centered programs. Planning for veterans had been confined during the war to the National Resources Planning Board, which the Republican opposition saw as the potential architect of a planned economy and which was killed by Congress in June 1943 after it had started to produce an American equivalent of the Beveridge Report. The administration's planning for rehabilitation of disabled veterans also earned disfavor by its attempt to confine their care to agencies dealing with the disabled population generally, and to direct their training toward areas of industry where it was projected that need for workers would exist under conditions of full employment.

A committee under Frederick Osborn studying postwar education of veterans similarly recommended that training benefits be limited to areas of industry projecting a need for trained workers, and budgetary concerns restricted the administration's proposal to one year of training plus a limited program of merit scholarships for up to three years more; the Office of Education and the Labor Department would be heavily involved in administration of the program. Unemployment benefits for veterans, in the administration's view, should be incorporated in a new federal unemployment system.

In December 1943, there were Senate hearings on the administration education bill, featuring unchecked quarreling among federal agencies. In January 1944, the American Legion published its own proposal, an omnibus bill covering a variety of subjects, almost all the provisions to be administered by the Veterans' Administration. The education benefits in the Legion's initial bill were limited to one year as of right plus a chance for an additional three years, but the limitation as to courses of study was rejected. The benefits were restricted to persons who had served for nine months or more and whose education had been interrupted, allowing them $300 per year for tuition and a living allowance of $50 for single students and $75 for married students. A title relating to home and farm loans was added; while the administration had considered the grant of small amounts of surplus lands to veterans, it had put forth no loan program. The unemployment benefits were simple: 52 weeks at $20 per week, to be administered, like virtually all the provisions of the bill, by the Veterans' Administration. The loan proposals called for 95 percent loans of up to $7,500 or $12,500 for farms, with the states to put up a dollar for every four federal dollars, and interest rates to be 1 percent on the federal share and 5 percent on the state share.

The Legion bill passed the Senate unanimously on March 24, 1944, with only minor revisions. Allowable tuition was raised to $500, the required period of military service was lowered from nine months to six, the requirement of interruption of education was eliminated as a condition of benefits, and only $1,000 of a loan was federally guaranteed, with an interest rate of 3 percent.

However, a House Committee under Rankin restored the "interruption" requirement for education benefits and limited unemployment benefits to 26 weeks; the loan guarantee amount was set at $1,500 with an allowable interest rate of 6 percent. The House diluted the "interruption" requirement by presuming interruption if the veteran had been in school within two years of induction and was under the age of 24 when inducted, and Rankin agreed to raise the loan guarantee to $2,500. After Rankin tried to deadlock the conference committee over the unemployment benefit provisions, which he did not wish to be made available to African-American servicemen in the rural South, the deadlock was broken when Congressman John Gibson, whose proxy Rankin held, was flown back to Washington for the crucial vote. The conference bill, approved by the House and Senate, provided for 52 weeks of unemployment benefits, raised the cut-off age for presumption of interrupted education to 25, and provided for $2,000 federal loan guarantees with a maximum interest rate of 4 percent and maximum term of 20 years. The monthly stipend for single students was $65 and for married students $90. President Roosevelt signed the bill on June 22, 1944. In December 1945, the act was amended by dropping the "interruption" provision and liberalizing the loan guarantees, which were set at $4,000 with a maximum term of 25 years; in 1950, the amount was raised to $7,500 or 60 percent of the loan, whichever was less, with a maximum term of 30 years. In 1948, student stipends were raised to $75 for single students, $105 for couples, and $120 for families.

The homes sold on VA mortgages in 1945 numbered 43,000 of the 324,900 built in that year, or 12.5%. In 1946, the liberalized guarantees raised the number of VA homes to 412,000 of the total production of 1,015,200 (40.5 percent), and in 1947 to 542,000 of 1,265,100 (42.8 percent). By 1950, the program still accounted for 498,000 of 1,908,100 homes (26 percent). Among World War II veterans, a total of 7.8 million had received education benefits, 2.2 million of them for attendance at two-year and four-year colleges, and 3,782,000 had benefited from the home loan program. Elaborate efforts to stimulate industrial and prefabricated housing for veterans failed; by 1947, Davis Ross wrote, "The only continuing element of veterans' housing could be found in […] the mortgage insurance system provided under the G. I. Bill of Rights in 1944."[19] One effect of the education benefits was to eliminate, at least for a time, the economic sorting of students among colleges. Because the $500 tuition allowance was higher than the tuition at even the best colleges, those students who could academically qualify flocked to them. Of the students using benefits at four-year colleges, 41 percent attended the 38 most prestigious institutions; the remaining 712 schools shared the remaining 59 percent.[20]

Underlying the success of these programs was the notion of reciprocity underlying them: in the words of Davis Ross,

> one by one the New Deal attempts to link indissolubly veterans' benefits with general needs of the population failed: the G. I. Bill of Rights emerged as a veterans' measure, rather than a direct subsidy to education or home building.[21]

The Korean GI Bill of Rights did not have the same effects. From 1955 to 1977, newly discharged veterans were provided with a stipend from which tuition had to be paid. This was payable for one-and-a-half months for each month of service up to a maximum of 45 months, the adjusted value of which in 2003 was $376 per month for those with no dependants, $448 with one dependant, and $510 with two dependants. Of those enrolling in colleges, only 20 percent enrolled in private colleges, as against 52 percent of their World War II counterparts.[22] From 1977 to 1985, no fixed amount was provided by statute; the education benefits were permitted to be varied by regulation and focused so as to be used as a recruiting tool. The basic scheme provided for 36 months of benefits. Individual servicemen could contribute up to $2,700 to the scheme, which the government would match in a 2:1 ratio; maximum contributors thus could get an extra $225 per month in benefits. Since 1985, a new scheme has been in place: those with three years' service were provided $900 per month in 2003 and $985 in 2004; those with two years' service received $732 in 2003 and $800 in 2004. Voluntary contributions matched by the government can add about $150 per month to these figures.

Those waiving educational assistance on enlistment get an extra $100 per month in base pay for 12 months. Those in technical schools with high tuition can receive 60 percent of tuition over a shorter period.[23] There was a later further liberalization sponsored by Senator James Webb.

In summarizing the lessons to be drawn from the GI Bill, Theda Skocpol, generally known as a champion of state programs, has observed, in a discussion of "The G.I. Bill and U.S. Social Policy": "the G.I. Bill fits the mould of many successful U.S. social policies; it encompassed both more and less privileged Americans, and it joined benefits with service, citizenship rewards with citizenship responsibilities."[24] In this, it resembled Morrill's design for land grant colleges, from which it was descended.

7

John Wesley Powell and Western Public Lands

John Wesley Powell was Director of the Rocky Mountain region of the US Geological Survey. He undertook a survey of arid lands of the West that convinced him that the noble provisions of the Homestead Act and its successors simply did not work in arid lands west of the 100th parallel of longitude. Attempts to take up homestead grants, even those for the enlarged tracts authorized by later legislation, were more productive of personal tragedy than successful settlement. The history of the Dakotas and places like Western Nebraska, Eastern Colorado, and Montana has been a history of stagnation or depopulation since the railroad booms of the 1880s and 1890s.

Powell was said to have been:

> a somewhat rough and striking figure. He was hearty and eminently magnetic, at times given to enforcing his views with military arbitrariness. He had a remarkable faculty for leadership and was likeable in the extreme. In his administration he gave every man a chance to demonstrate his capacity and was thus instrumental in launching the careers of a number of younger men who later attained distinction. He was always accessible to the least of his subordinates and interested in their welfare. His retirement from the leadership of the [Geological] Survey was brought about in part by antagonism to his forest preservation and irrigation projects.[1]

15. Major John Wesley Powell (Library of Congress)

He was also described as:

> small, crippled and unhandsome. His progenitors had been labor-
> ers and craftsmen. He was a first-generation American, the son of
> bigoted Calvinists, the product of a backwoods farm environment,
> self-educated and poor. [...] He dressed plainly and lived simply. Not
> infrequently his gray hair was in need of trimming. He had too much
> stomach and his scraggly gray beard, reaching to his vest, was stained
> by droppings from the scores of cigars which he chewed assiduously
> throughout each day. His linens were immaculate, but a suit that was
> clean and well-pressed in the morning might well be a mass of wrin-
> kles and pattered with ink stains and cigar ashes by noon.[2]

He was born in 1834, and studied at Illinois College, Wheaton
College, and Oberlin. As a young man, he went on rowing

16. John Wesley Powell Memorial, West Rim Drive, between Grand
Canyon Village and Hermit Rest, Grand Canyon, Coconino County,
Arizona (Library of Congress)

expeditions down a number of major rivers, including the whole
length of the Mississippi from Minnesota to New Orleans in
1856. During the Civil War, he lost most of an arm at the Battle
of Shiloh and was troubled by the injury for the rest of his life.
After the war, which he ended not as a major but a brevet colonel,
he became Professor of Geology at Illinois Wesleyan. In 1869,
he organized an expedition to explore the Colorado River, three
members of which lost their lives in an Indian attack. He repeated
the expedition in 1871–2, and published a report of it in 1875. In
1874, he organized a discussion group, which became the Cosmos
Club of Washington, DC. In 1881, he became the second director of the US Geological Survey and director of the Bureau of
Ethnology at the Smithsonian Institution.

    In 1878, Powell sent to his superiors a report on arid lands
together with proposed legislation.[3] The report included two bills.
The first would have authorized the creation of irrigation districts
by any nine or more persons where land required irrigation and
there was a water source sufficient to irrigate 320 acres.[4] Each

person could claim no more than 80 acres. The effort was to foster
the creation of cooperative irrigation districts: "Lands should be
actively irrigated before the title is transferred to the purchaser."[5]

A second bill authorized the creation of pasturage districts by
nine or more persons, each of whom could select 2,560 acres of
contiguous land that was not arable without irrigation.[6] Each person could select no more than two parcels, one no larger than 20
acres, for irrigation. No one person was entitled to water for irrigation exceeding that necessary for 20 acres, "nor shall the tract
be selected in such a manner along a stream as to monopolize a
greater amount." "[A]n equitable division of the waters can be
made only by a wise system of parcelling the lands; and the people
in organized bodies can well be trusted with this right, while individuals could not thus be trusted."[7] This suggestion for individual
ownership of two lots, one at the center of a town and one at the
periphery, is found in Plato's *Laws*, as Lewis Mumford pointed
out; it is unclear whether this was the antecedent of Powell's
proposal.[8]

Powell explained:

> it is essential that the residences be grouped to the greatest possible
> extent. This may be practically accomplished by making the pas-
> turage farms conform to topographic features in such manner as to
> give them the greatest possible number of water fronts. For the use
> of large streams, cooperative labor or capital is necessary. The small
> streams should not be made to serve lands so as to interfere with the
> use of the large streams.
>
> [...]
>
> As the pasturage lands will not usually be fenced, herds must
> roam in common. As the pasturage lands should have water fronts
> and irrigable tracts and as the residents should be grouped and as the
> lands cannot be economically fenced and must be kept in common,
> local regulations or cooperation is necessary.[9]

Wallace Stegner observed that "these lands could be settled and
improved by the 'colony plan' better than any other [...] Whole
complexes of cooperative institutions [...] in the 20th century have
made Alberta and Saskatchewan virtually socialist provinces."[10]

This was, for Powell, "essentially the lesson of all the mining district organizations of the west."[11] Powell favored cooperative private ownership of grazing lands, without which:

> no incentive is given to the improvement of the country and no legal
> security to pasturage rights. Those areas where water is available have
> been settled from an early date; the rest, which might legitimately
> have been attached to watered home ranches as grazing land, has
> remained in the hands of the federal government and is leased as
> range.[12]

While this design would require departure from the grid pattern beloved of land surveyors,

> it matters not what the shape of the tracts or parcels may be, if these
> parcels are accurately defined by surveys on the ground and platted
> for record, none of these uncertainties will arise and if these tracts or
> parcels are lettered or numbered on the plats, they may very easily be
> described in conveyances without entering into a long and tedious
> description of metes and bounds.
> [...]
> The title to no tract of land should be conveyed from the govern-
> ment to the individual until the proper survey of the same is made
> and the plat prepared for record.[13]

Powell's preferred area already had some reflection in Texas law. The law inherited from Mexico provided for 4,470-acre grazing tracts on state-owned lands, reduced to 1,280 acres in 1880 but increased to 2,560 acres in 1887 and 5,120 acres in 1906.[14]

More than 40 percent of the land area of the United States requires irrigation for agriculture. Powell feared a condition in which control of the land would rest with water companies: "The right to use water should inhere in the land to be irrigated, and water rights should go with land titles," otherwise "water will become a property independent of the land and this property will be gradually absorbed by a few."[15]

The proposal was objected to by the Western railroads, which feared that it would discourage settlers and reduce their number, thereby interfering with the sales of railroad lands.

> The report was ignored or denigrated at the time but subsequently was regarded as a visionary basic document underlying reclamation efforts in the Western United States after 1900 [...] During his later years and after his death Powell was vilified by Western Senators and land developers. Powell's rational approach to public land policy and development which he attempted to impose through the Geological Survey rankled Western developers, and he was forced out of the Survey in 1894.[16]

It was claimed that:

> There would have been no disastrous dust bowls if Powell's recommendations had been carried out. There would have been no vast areas made forever useless by erosion. Watersheds would not have been destroyed, with the result that great floods carried away irreplaceable soil and created havoc and disaster in regions that might have contained bountiful farms and prosperous towns. The great high plains that supported uncountable millions of wild animals would not have been destroyed, for Powell would have prevented homesteading and farming in areas—and these contained millions of acres—to which water could not be supplied but which in their natural state were superb grazing lands for cattle and sheep.[17]

Powell's view was adopted by Theodore Roosevelt in his message to Congress of December 3, 1901, declaring: "In the arid states, the only right to water that should be recognized is that of use. In irrigation this right should attach to the land reclaimed and be inseparable therefrom."[18]

The last gasp of the homestead policy was the Newlands Act of 1902 creating the federal reclamation program to enlarge the area of irrigated lands, extended to Texas by an amendatory act in 1906. Powell had mapped possible dam sites while head of the Geological Survey; in the final event, every important river in the

West had at least one dam. In Powell's view, irrigation was the only means through which the West could support agriculture. The cost of dams was initially defrayed by sales of public land; later a revolving fund received the government's proceeds from sales of newly irrigated land. The Newlands Act required an eight-hour day on irrigation projects, barred use of "Mongolian" labor, and required that half of the reclaimed land be used for farming. In 1939, the act was amended to provide liberal land payment terms extending over 40 years. While the expert view was that a family farm could utilize no more than 80 acres of irrigated land, the statute provided that "No right to the use of water for land in private ownership shall be sold for a tract exceeding 160 acres to any one landowner."[19] This has been described as "one of the most significant measures in shaping the development of the West."[20] By 1951, 100,000 farms inhabited by nearly a half-million people had been established on lands made irrigable by the Bureau of Reclamation. Ultimately 600 dams were constructed, creating about 10 million acres of irrigated land, or about 15,000 square miles. Some 60 percent of the nation's vegetables and 25 percent of its fruits and nuts are grown on the land thus developed; the associated dams fuel 58 power plants furnishing 40 billion kilowatts of electricity, and supply water to about one-third of the population of the Western states. A total of 5 percent of the land in the Western states is irrigated; one-fifth of the irrigated land was created as such by the Newlands Act.

The effect of the 160-acre restriction, which has always been controversial, has been limited in several respects. The limitation was inapplicable to reclamation projects carried out by the Army Corps of Engineers. Senator Patrick McCarran of Nevada for years waged guerilla warfare against the enforcement capabilities of the Bureau of Reclamation. There were also large land tracts in California dating from the Spanish and Mexican era whose owners constituted a powerful lobby and which inevitably derived incidental benefit from reclamation projects. The historian Paul W. Gates referred to "the great concentration of ownership of agricultural land that has continued into the twentieth century, the high average size and consequent smaller number of farms and the large number of farmers who owned no land."[21] "There is not a man in California who does not know how the ownership of these large tracts [Mexican land grants of 50,000–100,000 acres] has steadily retarded the progress and development of the state."[22] In California, Gates wrote in 1993, 264 persons own 25 percent of the land: "the great land companies are in effective political and economic control of California."[23] The journalist John Gunther had noted in 1947 that "Two percent of California landowners control one-fourth the acreage and nearly one-third of the crop value of the state."[24] The 160-acre limitation was essentially destroyed by the Reagan Administration's Reclamation Reform Act of 1982, which raised the acreage limit to 960 acres, abolished the residence requirement, preserved the Corps of Engineers exception, and allowed owners of larger tracts to buy water at full cost.[25] Further reclamation projects were discouraged by environmentalist opposition, which intensified after failure of the future Teton Dam in Wyoming in 1976, and resulted in a "hit list" of water projects prepared during the Carter Administration.

The Taylor Grazing Act of 1934:

> fifty-six years after Powell submitted his report to Schurz finally solved the problem of the dry land homesteaders by partially closing the public domain and it partially solved the problem of the cattlemen in need of extensive range by a system of grazing leases administered by the Bureau of Land Management. [...] [O]f the 400 million acres in the states of Montana, Wyoming, Colorado, Utah, Idaho and Nevada, more than half are still federally owned and managed. The west relies on a degree of federal paternalism that it is not always happy to accept.

It was said in 1924 that:

> In the semi-arid districts [...] a good range is spoiled for a bad grain field, and the grain field cannot readily be turned back into range. [...] [T]he government, states included, may well cease helping to create from year to year a new crop of sub-marginal farmers. To get sub-marginal land out of the farming category, and into a use for which it is fitted, would be a worthy goal in a land policy at once desirable and attainable.[26]

It has also been said that:

> A later judgment of the damage done to the public rangelands by
> the Enlarged Homestead and the Stock Raising Homestead Acts was
> that 50 million acres of land relatively good for grazing but sub-
> marginal for crops had gone to private ownership. Of this quantity
> 25 million acres had been abandoned for cultivation and 11 million
> acres additional now constituted "acute problem areas". On all this
> area the range had been destroyed and will be of little use for years to
> come unless reseeded.[27]

According to Peffer:

> Unregulated expansion into a region meant by nature to be range
> country did serious, often irreparable damage to the land. Though
> the passing of the frontier and the closing of the public domain were
> not simultaneous, it might have been better for the country if they
> more nearly coincided.[28]

The milestones in the reduction of the public domain from
557 million acres in 1900 (down from the original area of
1,442,000,000 acres, or more than 2 million square miles) to
170 million acres in 1950, of which 150 million was grazing land
under lease, can be described as follows: In 1877, the Desert Land
Act allowed homestead entries on parcels of 640 acres, reduced
to 320 acres in 1893.[29] In 1903–5, a Public Lands Commission
called for grazing leases, but noted that fencing increases the carrying capacity of grazing land. This pressure for retention of government ownership was for a time undone by new enthusiasm
for "dry farming," in which alternate fields were plowed up and
allowed to lie fallow to increase their absorptive capacity. Twice
as much land was needed for each farmer engaged in "dry farming," which did not live up to expectations. Homestead tracts of
640 acres were provided for by the Enlarged Homestead Act of
1909 and the Stock Grazing Homestead Act of 1916. In 1909–10
alone, 18 million acres were withdrawn from the public domain.
Most of the tracts were found to be non-viable as homesteads and
were sold to large cattle operators.

The Taylor Grazing Act of 1934 all but cut off homesteading by reducing the maximum area to 320 acres and by withdrawing lands for reclassification.

Very small homesteads of five acres were provided for by the Small Tract Law of 1938, which was repealed in 1976; its beneficiaries were required to erect not homes but small cabins with a minimum size of 192 square feet. Some 457,000 acres of land were offered, and about 150,000 acres were patented. Half the patents were in California. Ronald Reagan was one of the original applicants in 1945, though he never perfected his claim; Frank Sinatra was awarded a patent in 1959. The residue of the project consists of checkerboard development, including, as of 2004, 2,500 abandoned shacks.[30]

The Taylor Act was enacted after the failure of a Hoover Administration proposal to transfer the remaining public domain to the states. Instead, the states were given a portion of lease proceeds.[31] The Federal Land Policy and Management Act of 1976 confirmed Bureau of Land Management and Forest Service ownership of the remaining public domain. The lax enforcement of grazing restrictions led Paul W. Gates to estimate that "75% of the range [was] producing less than half of its forage potential," and to urge exclusion of domestic livestock from grazing on frail lands: "Holders of the 21,000 grazing permits virtually dictated federal policy on the BLM rangelands including the fees they paid."[32] The Homestead Act was finally repealed in 1976, with a ten-year grace period for Alaska.

This history lends credence to James Bryce's reflections about the Western states a century ago:

> the political point of view—the fact that they were the founders of new commonwealths and responsible to posterity for the foundations they laid, a point so trite and obvious to a European visitor that he pauses before expressing it—had not crossed their minds [...] [T]here is in their words a further evidence of the predominance of material effects and interests over all others, even over those political instincts which are deemed so essential a part of the American character. The arrangements of his government lie in the dim background of the picture which fills the Western eye [...] These are the shadows

which to the eye of the traveller seem to fall across the glowing land-scape of the Great West.[33]

A Powell biographer observed that "Democracy survived in the United States because natural resources were too vast to be completely stolen and destroyed before a few honourable public-spirited men could obtain enough authority to control the plundering."[34]

While Powell's design for irrigated areas was not accepted, the ownership requirement and 160-acre limitation in the Newlands Act gave rise to a wide dispersion of ownership of irrigated lands, from which their half-million residents benefited greatly. Lake Powell on the Arizona–Nevada border is named after him; there is a memorial museum in Page, Arizona.

Powell was noted also for his ethnographic work, which was informed by the same moral insights about the importance of relating work to land as his geological survey work. It was said of the 40 volumes he and his co-workers assembled about the Western Indians that "the philosophy of history is being erected out of materials accumulating by objective studies of mankind [...] among the most important contributions to human history ever made by an individual, an institution, or a state."[35] On the basis of these studies, he condemned much of the nation's policy toward Native Americans, which have oscillated between paternalism and plunder. He thought that reservations should be "schools of industry [...] no able-bodied Indian should be fed or clothed except as payment for labour." He considered that Native Americans should be encouraged to make their own garments, and urged the establishment on reservations of artisans with Native American apprentices and that families each be given a cow for subsistence, together with training in English. Policy should be removed from factions, "one crying for blood and the other that the progress of civilization may be stayed."[36] He considered that "Government does not begin in the ascendancy of chieftains through prowess in war but in the slow specialization of executive functions from communal associations based on kinship. Councils precede chieftains." He was no adherent of laissez-faire:

The preceding theories of political economy became popular at a time when governments were unpopular, which is not now the case because they have become more representative in form. Former attempts at governmental regulation were impractical because they sought to control opinion.[37]

8

Joseph Pulitzer and Municipal Home Rule

Joseph Pulitzer (1847–1911) is best remembered as the proprietor of the *St. Louis Post Dispatch* and for the Pulitzer Prizes. It is not remembered that in his youth, as a Missouri legislator, he was the first successful American champion of municipal home rule.

He was born in Hungary and came to the United States at the age of 17 as a recruit for the Union Army in the American Civil War. He served for eight months in the First New York Lincoln Cavalry. On arrival, he spoke only German, Hungarian, and French. After the war, he proceeded to St. Louis by railroad boxcar; it is said that he went there as a result of a misunderstood joke. A friend of his told him that St. Louis was a good place to learn English; in fact it was notorious that the population was still largely German-speaking. Legend has it that he sold his only valuable possession, a white handkerchief, for 75 cents. After holding a number of odd jobs and studying English and law, he was admitted to the Missouri bar in 1868 at the age of 21, but had few clients. He became a reporter for the *Westliche Post* in the same year. He joined the Republican Party and at a party meeting on December 14, 1869, he was recruited to run for the state legislature. He was elected over a possibly ineligible ex-Confederate by a vote of 209–147 and was seated in the legislature, which overlooked the fact that at 22 he was three years under the minimum age. There he became involved in a brawl with a lobbyist in which shots were fired, but no criminal charges were pressed against him.[1]

17. Portrait of United States publisher Joseph Pulitzer, 1918
(Public domain)

It was said of the young Pulitzer during this period that:

> He certainly stood out. He was the only one to have his photograph
> taken with a hat on, cocked ever so slightly to his right. It was a slouch
> hat, a style introduced to the United States by the revolutionary leader
> Louis Kossuth when he fled Hungary. Along with this hat, Pulitzer
> wore a pince-nez, a mustache, a narrow pointed goatee trimmed in a
> style known as a Napoleon III and a royale (a tuft of hair under the
> lower lip)—if he was seeking to be noticed, he succeeded.[2]

Later he was a delegate to the national convention of the Liberal
Republican party which nominated Horace Greeley. In the 1870
session, he unsuccessfully strove to reform the county court that
exercised supervision over St. Louis, subjecting it to a costly dual

18. The *fin de siècle* newspaper proprietor (Library of Congress)

system of government. Since the consolidation of the city with the county or its separation from it would each require a constitutional amendment, Pulitzer instead tried to reconstruct the county court, by replacing the existing seven-member county court with a nine-member court with six city members. The bill was amended to provide a five-member court with three city members, a county member, and an at-large member, but failed to be enacted.[3] In 1869, the county government had undertaken the construction of an insane asylum that incurred massive cost overruns, including those for a water-less well, which at 3,850 feet became the second-deepest shaft in the world and was described by Pulitzer as the "well of fools."[4] In 1871, a renewed effort gave rise to a new seven-member court, two each from the city and the county and three members at large. After the governor called for a constitutional convention, one was duly elected to take office in 1875. Twelve delegates were elected from St. Louis. Disgusted with corruption during the Grant Administration, Pulitzer became a Democrat and in 1880 was elected to the Democratic National Convention and was a member of its platform committee. In 1884, after acquiring the *New York World*, he was elected to the US House of Representatives from the 9th District of New York, but resigned after a year because of the demands of journalism. He became one of nine Democrats sent by St. Louis to the convention.[5]

In the period 1871–5, 51 special laws applicable only to the City of St. Louis were adopted by the Missouri legislature. It was said that "the 'charter' of St. Louis was contained in a conglomeration of one hundred separate state statutes, some of them of formidable length."[6]

In 1875, at the age of 28, Pulitzer was elected as a St. Louis delegate to the Missouri constitutional convention, where the St. Louis delegates expressed disgust at the "transitory nature of the municipal structure and the ease with which amendments and revisions passed through the legislature."[7] "[Boss William Marcy] Tweed [of New York] derived all his power and based his entire system of public plunder on such an amendment as is proposed. The power of Tweed and his coadjutors lay in making charters in Albany and in carrying out charters in New York."[8] The 1875 convention, elected in the wake of the Panic of 1873, was one in which:

> a cautious and conservative point of view was dominantly held and expressed by a large majority of the convention membership. Nearly half of the delegates were men well past middle age [...] It is surprising and paradoxical, therefore, that a convention so permeated by conservatism and so thoroughly distrustful of constitutional innovations would sanction in the new fundamental law a plan which [quoting Howard Lee Mc Bain] "marked the most important step that had ever been taken in the United States in the direction of securing home rule to cities through the medium of a constitutional provision. [It] exemplified something of the pioneer's daring originality of spirit in the matter of political institutions," and has served as a guide to more than one-fourth the states of the Union in their attempt "by this somewhat heroic method to liberate their cities from the dominating influence of the legislature."[9]

Pulitzer was appointed to the committee on boundaries and political subdivisions, where he sought the appointment of a special committee to consider the affairs of St. Louis, "a small state by itself," with a population of a half-million, paying half the state's taxes, with a local debt larger than the state's debt:

We merely ask that the representatives of St. Louis be awarded the privilege of considering their own interests and their own duties [...] [T]he Convention will certainly have wisdom enough to pass as a court of last resort upon any recommendations that the Committee might make.[10]

After the proposal was slightly modified, a Committee on St. Louis Affairs was approved.

On the ninth day of the convention, Pulitzer presented a resolution with five branches limiting official salaries to $10,000 per year, providing for at-large election of the St. Louis legislative delegation, providing for compulsory education, and separating St. Louis from the surrounding county. The fifth branch of the resolution provided for a municipal charter that was amendable only by the mayor, two-thirds of the council, and two-thirds of the people voting in an election to amend the charter.[11] Pulitzer's "pertinacity and his energy would certainly be employed to secure recognition for his ideas and to incorporate them in the new constitution."[12] He proposed that municipalities of 100,000 or more inhabitants "shall be regulated by a fundamental constitutional charter which shall not be liable to yearly change by the Legislature, but shall remain a permanent fundamental law of the State."[13] Amendment would require the assent of the mayor and two-thirds of the city council, and would have to be "endorsed by at least two-thirds of the people thereof voting at a special election." "In Pulitzer's opinion, such a system would prove a formidable bastion against the perceived villains of the urban drama."[14] It was said that "there is scarcely an amendment made to the charter that does not cost the city not only thousands but hundreds of thousands of dollars." The city was said to have been "blown over by every wind and flood of bummerism, high fraud and rascally speculators."[15] Pulitzer's proposal was adopted, a three-fifths rather than two-thirds majority of voters being required, a savings clause being included that made clear that the legislature retained the same power over St. Louis "as it has over other cities and counties" in the state. It followed that "St. Louis was the first city in the United States to frame its own charter."[16]

The city unsuccessfully attempted to gain additional seats in the legislature, but was not aided in this effort by what were described as "the provocative and sarcastic remarks of the ubiquitous Pulitzer."[17] Although the energetic advocates of home rule were initially a small minority in the St. Louis delegation, they had unusual "ability and perseverance." An amendment that would have allowed the legislature to amend the municipal charter was vigorously opposed by Pulitzer:

> give over to us those matters of business and vital necessity to the City of St. Louis. Do not interfere, let us govern ourselves, carry out the true principles of local self-government; that is all we want [...] Give us something we understand, that we can control ourselves, and give us something which no one who has no right to do so can take away from us.[18]

According to Barclay, "These unequivocal statements, delivered with Pulitzer's customary assurance, aroused apprehension among his colleagues."[19] Their concerns were propitiated by allowing the charter to be supplanted by general laws but not by laws special to St. Louis. There was a specific prohibition of special legislation for municipal affairs.

Pulitzer's Missouri language was copied virtually word for word in a California Constitution adopted in 1881.[20] In 1889, the provisions were copied in Washington State (where only a simple majority of voters was required to amend) and in 1896 in Minnesota, in 1902 in Colorado, in 1906 in Oregon, in 1907 in Oklahoma, and in 1908 in Michigan.[21] By 1920, 20 of the 33 American cities with a population of more than 200,000 enjoyed municipal home rule;[22] by 1923, virtually all of them did. In 1894, the National Municipal League was founded to foster the cause of municipal home rule,[23] and promulgated model constitutional amendments, charters, and laws in 1899.[24] Pulitzer later, in 1881, had second thoughts about the rigidity of St. Louis's municipal charter restrictions on bond issues (by 1890, 14 states had constitutional restrictions on municipal debt),[25] and in 1902 the Constitution was amended to require only three-fifths of voters on a proposition rather than three-fifths voting at the election to approve charter amendments. The restrictions against special laws remained in full force; in 1885, the Missouri legislature abolished its special committee for St. Louis bills. Before home rule amendments,

> State interference had reached such an extent that the New York legislature passed more municipal laws in the three years between 1867 and 1870 than the entire total in England for the 50 years from 1835 to 1885. There were 39 state laws for Brooklyn alone in 1870.[26]

It was said that "In the twentieth century, home rule advocates were suspicious of state lawmakers, in the 1870s they had feared all lawmakers. [...] They introduced a lawmaking procedure that was to assume new importance in the twentieth century."[27] It curbed the abuses readily perpetrated by a handful of legislators in remote state capitols in favor of a sometimes disorderly brokering among groups at the municipal level, which "balanced the elements within society and provided the services vital to citizens in the industrialized world of the late nineteenth century."[28] The Supreme Court in 1893 referred to the Missouri amendment as establishing an *"imperium in imperio."*[29] All but a half-dozen states have now adopted one form or another of home rule amendments; the earlier ones accord courts the power to define municipal powers; since 1962, the later ones, designed by the late Dean Jefferson Fordham of the University of Pennsylvania Law School, have accorded a greater role to state legislatures.[30] It has been asserted that courts have largely vitiated these grants of municipal power,[31] though this contention has been vigorously disputed.[32] There is no American equivalent of the European Charter of Local Self-Government, or of the new general competence granted to British local governments by the new 2011 Localism Act.

Pulitzer's home rule amendment proved not to be an unmixed blessing for St. Louis. The rigid separation of city and county that resulted from it precluded further annexations and limited the City's tax base, leading one writer to declare that it gave St. Louis the "status of a medieval walled town,"[33] and another to assert that, "[b]arred from annexing land and facing severe constitutional restrictions on raising taxes, the city would, over time, become impoverished, deserted by its wealthier citizens, and transformed into a destitute urban core surrounded by a wealthy county."[34] The boundary provisions, however, are conceptually separable from the "home rule" provisions, and do not discredit them. A proposed amendment in 1924 to allow annexation or merger was rejected by the electorate. The Home Rule provision continued to confine control of St. Louis's elections and police to state-appointed boards; the police board is said to have kept policing out of politics. The city's efforts to regulate public utilities were generally held to have been pre-empted by the state's general laws. However, the intent of the provision was respected, the Missouri Supreme Court ruling in 1894 that municipal laws, to be valid, had to be consistent only with state "laws of general rather than local concern."[35]

At the Missouri convention, Pulitzer also eloquently expressed some broader convictions:

> I believe that the State of Missouri desires for her citizens at least the capacity to write their own names and to be able to read before they vote in a government that should be based on intelligence and not ignorance.
>
> [...]
>
> Poverty is not as great a danger to liberty as is wealth with its corrupting demoralizing influences. Let us have prosperity but never at the expense of liberty, never at the expense of real self-government, and let us never have a government at Washington owing its retention to the power of the millionaires rather than to the will of the millions.[36]

When he departed from Missouri politics, he began his remarkable later career. In 1872, he had bought and sold the *Westliche Post* at a profit. In 1879, he bought the *St. Louis Dispatch* and the *St. Louis Post* and merged them to create the *St. Louis Post Dispatch*. In 1883, he bought the *New York World* for $346,000 from Jay Gould. The paper was accused of practicing "yellow journalism" and included "illustrations, advertising and a culture of consumption for working men." In 1909, after his papers exposed a payment of $40 million to the French Panama Canal Company by the US government, he was indicted for assertedly libeling President Roosevelt and J.P. Morgan; the indictments were ultimately dismissed. On his death in 1911, he left a fortune of $30 million, a sum equal to 1/1142nd of the gross national product as of the date of his death, a fortune equivalent to those of today's Bill Gates and Warren Buffett.[37] On his retirement, he declared a faith to which his newspapers usually but not always adhered:

> I know that my retirement will make no difference in its cardinal principles, that it will always fight for progress and reform, never tolerate injustice or corruption, always fight demagogues of all parties, never belong to any party, always oppose privileged classes and public plunderers, never lack sympathy with the poor, always remain devoted to the public welfare, never be satisfied with merely printing news, always be drastically independent, never be afraid to attack wrong, whether by predatory plutocracy or predatory poverty.[38]

American cities and their residents take for granted their wide discretion in enacting new municipal ordinances, contracting debt and enacting taxes, appointing their own department heads, and restructuring public services. The authorities would be vitiated if cities and their officials were subject to a steady bombardment of "ripper bills" curbing or evicting controversial officers and capricious alterations of authority and reversals of local decisions emanating from small coteries in a frequently remote state capital. The problems of American city government largely arise from the erosion of manufacturing tax bases and from unwise ukases from on high relating to crime and education. They would retain no civic vitality at all but for the efforts of a remarkable young state legislator in 1875.

One commentator views the 25 years beginning in 1895 as the Golden Age of American municipal government:

In retrospect, it has become clear that the grant-in-aid was a potent device in its accelerating and focusing efforts. Whether in the long run it was wise as an over-all policy is today under fire. As a financially equalizing device for poorer areas it had a clear role. As a general policy, given adequate municipal resources, the case for it was certainly not apparent in 1920. The cities were still eager to advance by their own efforts in all their traditional fields as well as in many new ones. The multiplication of functions on the part of cities indicated that they had little need to be stimulated to the exercise of their powers, so long as the property tax rate could be raised from time to time. The value of such local spontaneous effort should not be under-rated. My own hope for our cities is that they shall become free again, not from the old coercion but from the more subtle long-range effects of subsidies. Freedom can be undermined by the temptation and bribery of conditional grants-in-aid. With this freedom would come renewed clarity of responsibility. The ultimate wisdom of education through free internally financed self-government in the municipality has few better illustrations than the years 1895–1920.[39]

Ironically, municipal home rule in most states operates to quench the formation of sub-municipal special districts, which can usually be readily formed in rural areas but the creation of which is usually anathema to existing municipal bureaucracies. Nearly all states, however, under pressures from the business community and their more well-heeled citizens, have authorized the creation of business improvement districts[40] and historic preservation districts. The first make available to inner-city businesses the cooperative provision of advertising, parking, decoration, and security characteristic of suburban shopping centers;[41] the second provide established neighborhoods with the aesthetic controls customary in new developments. There remains considerable scope for other instrumentalities, including large-scale residential improvement districts, several of which exist in Baltimore, and smaller-scale precinct-level organizations,[42] like the British parish councils that recent legislation now permits to be organized in urban as well as rural areas.[43] The need for a comprehensive level of sub-local instrumentalities has recently received dramatic recognition in India, with the addition in 1993 of Amendments 73 and 74 to the Indian Constitution, requiring the creation throughout India of new village and ward governments with resources sufficient "to enable them to function as institutions of self-government."

9

Hugh Hammond Bennett and Soil Conservation Districts

There are today in the United States more than 3,000 local conservation districts (soil conservation districts in most states, natural resource or resource conservation districts in some). In 1992, these districts received about $500 million in state and local revenues, an amount that has since increased, and had at least 7,000 full-time employees and 17,000 part-time board members, numbers that compare favorably with the approximately 12,000 employees of the federal Natural Resources Conservation Service (NRCS) (formerly the Soil Conservation Service (SCS) until it was renamed by the Clinton Administration in 1994 in consequence of the Federal Crop Insurance Reform and Department of Agriculture Reorganization Act of 1994). The districts have attained this growth without benefit of any dedicated revenue sources, state or federal (although in Nebraska, almost uniquely, they receive 1 percent of property taxes). By 1964, 98 percent of the nation's farmland was situated in districts, which covered a land area of 1,060 million acres or about one-and-a-half million square miles, half the land area of the United States.[1] These districts were organized on local initiative, requiring citizen petitions, under 50 different state enabling laws. Although the federal government used various forms of suasion to promote the enactment of the state laws, including favoring states with "adequate" laws in the location of Civilian Conservation

19. Hugh Hammond Bennett (Public domain)

20. Dust Storm, 1935. Ada, Idaho Soil Conservation District
(http://adaswcd.org/ada-swcd-2/history)

Corps (CCC) camps, organization of districts has never been an express condition of federal aid to states and the districts receive no federal funds.

The man responsible for this rather striking civic development is little remembered outside his specialized field of endeavor.

21. Hugh Hammond Bennett Memorial (Public domain)

Hugh Hammond Bennett has been the subject of a biography by Worthington Brink,[2] a biographical sketch by Jonathan Daniels,[3] and a few obituaries and encyclopedia treatments,[4] but figures in few standard history texts. He was said to have combined the roles of "fiery apostle, practical leader and chronicler."[5] A not-uncritical commentator declared that:

> The Soil Conservation Service has had magnificent leadership, a truly charismatic leader in Max Weber's terms […] Bennett has made the Soil Conservation Service program a crusade: its members are dedicated […] SCS has not merely a staff, it has a corps and an esprit de corps, a goal, a body of dogma—indeed it has fired the imagination of a number of followers with that trilogy of authority, mystery and miracles celebrated by Dostoevsky's Grand Inquisitor in *The Brothers Karamazov*.[6]

He was described as a "rumpled figure, pockets bulging with notes and clippings, necktie askew, and hair mussed. His shoes were muddy from early morning garden work."[7] Elsewhere he was described as having a "gray fringe of hair wild in air, trouser cuffs drooping, necktie askew, vest partly unbuttoned."[8] Among his eccentricities were that he never learned to use a typewriter or to drive a car other than the Model T. In the course of his career he claimed to have visited every county in the nation with the exception of perhaps three in northern Michigan, north-eastern Nevada, and Oregon.[9]

Bennett joined the Bureau of Soils in the Department of Agriculture after graduating from the University of North Carolina in 1903; he had left college for two years, for economic reasons, and worked in a small-town drug store, a valuable experience. His early work was as a chemist classifying soil types under a director, Milton Whitney, chief of the Bureau of Soils, who in 1909 proclaimed that "soil is the one resource that cannot be exhausted, cannot be used up."[10]

In 1905, Bennett observed the phenomenon he called "sheet erosion," the washing away of topsoil, which led him later to state of the director's declaration: "I didn't know so much costly misinformation could be put into a single brief sentence."[11] His views did not earn him favor. In 1909 he received a small promotion, becoming chief of soil surveys for the 18-state Southern Region. Thereafter, however, he was banished to remote surveys in the Panama Canal Zone, Costa Rica, and Panama in 1909 and 1913; in Alaska in 1914 and 1916 working on the Alaska Railway and the Chugatch National Forest; in Cuba in 1925–6 and 1928; in Ecuador, Venezuela, and Brazil studying rubber cultivation in 1923–4 (producing a book-length study entitled *Possibilities for Para Rubber Production in Northern Tropical America*, and losing 40 pounds in the process); and to the Guatemala–Honduras border in 1919. In 1944, he visited South Africa.[12] While in Cuba studying sugar cultivation, he urged that plantation workers use stubble mulching rather than burning, and that they be permitted to grow their own food, which would minimize transient labor. He published *Agricultural Possibilities of the Canal Zone* in 1912; *Soil Renaissance in Alaska* in 1915, and (with R. Allison) *Soils of Cuba* in 1928, for which he was decorated by the Cuban government. In 1921, he published a work on *Soils of the South*. He had to reach outside his bureau to find an audience for his views on soil conservation, giving an important paper to the Southern Forestry Association in 1921.

He became a columnist for *Farm Journal* in 1925–6 and also wrote for *Nature*, the *North American Review*, *Scientific Monthly*, and *Country Gentleman*, among other publications. In 1928, following the great Mississippi Valley floods, he made a breakthrough to national prominence by publishing with W.R. Chapline of the Forest Service a monograph entitled *Soil Erosion: A National Menace* (USDA Circular 33). He wrote texts on *Costs of Soil Erosion* (1934), *Soil Conservation* (1939), and *Elements of Soil Conservation* (1947). With the help of Congressman John Buchanan of Texas, in 1929 Bennett was successful in obtaining an appropriation of $160,000 over four years to "investigate the causes of soil erosion and the possibility of increasing the absorption of rainfall by the soil in the United States." Ten erosion stations were established around the country, and in 1930 Bennett delivered the findings at the annual convention of the American Society of Agronomy.

When the Civilian Conservation Corps was established by the Roosevelt Administration in 1933, Bennett noted that $5 million of its appropriation was earmarked for erosion control to be administered by the Bureau of Agricultural Engineering. With the aid of Assistant Secretary of Agriculture Rexford Guy Tugwell, a member of Roosevelt's White House "brains trust," Bennett was able to secure the creation, by Interior Secretary Harold Ickes, of a Soil Erosion Service with himself as director, and by October 1933, 150 CCC camps had been transferred to it by the Forest Service. Forty large demonstration projects were created; by 1938, there were 162 demonstration projects and 324 CCC camps.[13] In December 1933, Secretary of Agriculture Henry Wallace urged the re-transfer of the SCS to his department, which was directed by President Roosevelt. In June 1935, an Inter-bureau Committee set up by Wallace attempted to mediate disputes between the new service and the Agricultural Extension Service attached to the land grant colleges. In the meantime, in April 1935 Bennett had been successful in securing permanent status for the SCS in a Soil Conservation Act signed in April 1935 (74th Congress, Public Law 46); the act had even been supported by former President

Hoover, who, however, wanted its powers to be given to the land grant colleges. At one point Bennett is said to have been interested in a Mussolini-era Italian law providing for forced cooperation of landowners and mandatory cost-sharing; the decision of the Supreme Court in the *Butler* case ended any interest in that idea.[14] The Supreme Court decision greatly aided the cause of soil conservation. By invalidating direct production restrictions, it caused energies to be diverted to a program of payments to farmers for:

> various methods of plowing and cultivation which would check erosion, to substitute grasses and legumes for soil-depleting crops such as cotton, tobacco, corn and wheat, and to practice soil-building with chemical fertilizers and in other ways. In return he received compensation out of the general funds of the Treasury for labor to check erosion which aided the national program or for the lease of land to the government. [...] The Court's decision might be said to have caused an expansion rather than an abandonment of the administration's agricultural program.[15]

Bennett became famous for his testimony at a congressional hearing; having been informed that a dust storm was about to strike Washington from the Midwest for only the second time in its history, he deliberately protracted his testimony until the dust storm made its appearance, and the Senators were directed to the windows. "For once, nature cooperated generously." The dust originated in an area encompassing Western Oklahoma, the Texas panhandle, Southwestern Kansas, Southeastern Colorado, and Northeastern New Mexico.

After two years of operation, only about a million acres of land had been treated by the new agency. As a measure to involve farmers, Bennett urged the creation of local Soil Conservation Districts centered on watersheds. These, he accurately foresaw, would be a political support for the SCS program. His biographer Wellington Brink described these as "pure invention, utterly without precedent [...] an historic departure from the modern trend toward government leadership and direction and control of private lives and enterprise."[16] A commentator later sardonically observed: "Humility respecting accomplishments of one's program is not a well-rewarded virtue on Capitol Hill. The upward trend in SCS appropriations has required great political acumen."[17] Because of doubts about federal authority, and because of the success of a similar approach carried out by Herbert Hoover as Secretary of Commerce to secure the enactment of zoning laws, a Standard State Soil Conservation Act was drafted and was sent to the state governors by President Roosevelt in February 1937. The act contemplated the formation of districts on petition by 25 farmers and a referendum election establishing boundaries. The model act contemplated referenda on contract proposals and contracts running with the land binding landowners, as well as the adoption of land-use regulations by the districts subject to referenda. Some 22 states adopted enabling laws by the end of 1937, the first district being established in Bennett's home county in Georgia. The role of the districts vis-à-vis the extension service was confirmed in what became known as the Mt. Weather Agreement on July 8, 1938. Nearly 15 years later, A. Whitney Griswold, then president of Yale, was to observe:

> All planning in connection with the new action programs was to begin in local communities with local committees [...] In an age in which the governments of the world have been steadily extending their powers over the economic life of nations, it was remarkable evidence of respect for the fundamental democratic principles of individual freedom and local self-government.[18]

States with statutes were favored in the placement of CCC camps. A number of states refused to adopt the provision authorizing land-use ordinances; others imposed a super-majority requirement for referenda. By 1938, there were 27 state laws, 12 of which were deemed satisfactory by the SCS and six of which contained no ordinance provisions; by 1947, all 48 continental states had laws. In June 1937, the SCS made it clear that ordinance provisions were not a condition for federal aid. At the same time, the SCS was involved in President Roosevelt's "shelterbelt" program, the president's own initiative. Originally conceived as a 100-mile wide belt of trees running from north to south for 1,000 miles through the Great Plains, it was whittled down into a series of isolated strings of trees; by 1943, when the program ran out of money with the end of the Works Progress Administration (WPA) and CCC there were more than 30,000 shelterbelts, more than 20,000 miles in length, containing upwards of 220 million trees.[19] By way of comparison, a much-vaunted international voluntary Global Re Leaf program boasted in 2008 that in the first 20 years of its existence, it had planted 25 million trees, hoping to plant 100 million by 2020.[20]

In 1937, a Committee on Long Range Programs and Policies presided over by Bennett laid down principles that would control the program for 25 years, including education, the combination of soil erosion prevention and flood control, cooperation with other agencies but separation from state extension services, service to individual landowners, and direct connection between the SCS and local committees without state intervention. In 1939, a major change resulted in the publication of simplified, standardized, and easy-to-understand Conservation Survey Maps, classifying land into eight categories, each depicted in a bright color.[21]

The number of districts grew from 462 in 1941, covering 262 million acres or about 400,000 square miles, to 700 in 1942 and 1,235 in 1944. By 1964 there were 1.9 million agreements with farmers, including 32 percent of farm operating units; districts covered 1,060 million acres or more than a million-and-a-half square miles; 98 percent of all farmland was in districts.[22] There was serious resistance to the establishment of districts only in California, a state of large landowners, and in some parts of Missouri, Oregon, and Pennsylvania. The SCS by 1945 had 8,224 full-time and 4,104 part-time employees. In September 1936, the program reached its peak size in terms of employees, employing 23,700 WPA workers.

The political character of the districts altered over time. Initially it was contemplated that they be organized on the basis of watersheds to separate them from county courthouse rings. Consideration of convenience gave rise to increased use of county units. Under pressure from Southern congressmen, land occupiers were deprived of votes in referenda, leading to the comment that "there is no damned nonsense about the plight of the sharecropper or of migratory labor in the area of policy with which SCS deals."[23]

On the other hand, the need to maintain congressional support was an impetus to keeping the SCS out of politics: its staff was almost entirely composed of civil servants and Bennett was its director for 16 years, outlasting all the Department of Agriculture's other agency heads and several Secretaries of Agriculture. The SCS gradually won its battle with the state extension services, which tended to over-emphasize research, and tended to be politically allied with the Roosevelt Administration's critics, particularly the American Farm Bureau Federation. The agency had an ebb and flow of functions; it was deprived of farm forestry but gained new authority over small watersheds and, in the Bankhead–Jones Act, to promote small farms. Its small watershed activity has sometimes produced conflicts with the Army Corps of Engineers, with its characteristic emphasis on large projects. In 1939, a Division of Irrigation and Drainage was created to deal with arid lands. A "shelterbelt" program was transferred to it in 1942 but later abandoned. In 1956, a Great Plains Conservation Program emphasizing grass cover was enacted; the SCS was also directed to compile an inventory of soil conservation needs, a task completed in 1961 with updates later.

Bennett initiated a highly publicized program of "farm face liftings," in which massive quantities of earth-moving equipment were brought to work on single farms, so as to accomplish five years' work in 24 hours; 100 such shows were conducted, attracting total audiences estimated at 2 million persons.[24]

Not all of the SCS's ventures were fully successful. One embarrassment was the kudzu distribution program from 1934 to 1953, which propagated "the weed that ate the South" as a soil preservative and nitrogen nutrient, but at the expense of much other vegetation.[25]

Bennett continued to propagandize for the cause and was the joint author of *This Land We Defend* in 1942.[26] This work alleged that 3 billion tons of soil were lost each year and that 25 percent of the run-off in a 500,000-square-mile area could be prevented. By 1944, the need for labor in defense plants brought an end to the use of CCC and WPA labor by the SCS in its "demonstration projects." A National Association of Soil Conservation Districts was organized in 1944 and became a powerful lobby for

SCS appropriations. Legislation in 1954 enjoined a fiscal separation between the SCS and districts, which were able to politically sustain themselves against the Eisenhower Administration's initial bias in favor of land grant colleges (including the one once presided over by the president's brother, Milton Eisenhower) and their extension services. Secretary Ezra Taft Benson eliminated the SCS's regional offices but strengthened state offices; an effort by the Kastenbaum Commission to convert the SCS into a grant-in-aid program to the states, which would have destroyed its *esprit de corps*, was stillborn.

The districts discovered that agreements with farmers were a more effective device than land-use regulations, which were promulgated by only about a dozen districts, most of them in Colorado. The Colorado regulations, aimed at preventing wind erosion, prohibited the plowing up of sod land. One North Dakota district sought to relate grazing rights to carrying capacity; an Oregon district enacted protective legislation for sand dunes.[27] The cause of land erosion prevention benefited from the conversion of much Southern land from cotton to forestry. The persistence of subsidies for wheat-growing meant that there was less change in the Great Plains, the center of the dust bowl problem. By legislation in 1994, the SCS was renamed the Natural Resources Conservation Service and was given mandates for water as well as land conservation and has become concerned with problems such as urban runoff. It has also become involved in the purchase of sub-marginal lands, in conservation easements, and in programs of maintenance payments to farmers withdrawing land from production in the interest of erosion control, an approach that has found much favor in England.[28]

Bennett reached retirement age in 1951; his tenure was extended for a year by executive order of President Truman. He received honorary degrees from Columbia, the University of North Carolina, and Clemson; the building now housing the NRCS was named after him. Two years after his retirement he urged the merger of the Agricultural Conservation Programs Branch and the SCS and protested against the movement of research functions to another agency. He regarded the soil survey work assigned to the SCS as a distraction and viewed with alarm a fall of a million acres in the area receiving services between 1950 and 1952. "As long as there is any possibility of helping to keep soil conservation properly aligned, I shall want to do what I can by flagging the plays that appear to be the wrong ones."[29] In the same period, the journalist Bernard De Voto viewed with alarm some of the policies of Eisenhower's Secretary of Agriculture Ezra Taft Benson, though he noted that the administration had backed off from efforts to abolish or transfer regional offices and research facilities. He noted that several top SCS officials had been removed from the career service and made Schedule C political appointees, and alleged that the role of the land grant colleges had been overly aggrandized. "Promising young men have left SCS in droves." He asserted, without specifics, that two dust bowls had formed: "The best place to get a Colorado farm is Eastern Kansas."[30] Bennett died in July 1960 and is buried in Arlington National Cemetery; his papers are in the Southern History Collection at the University of North Carolina, at the National Archives in Department of Agriculture Record Group 114, and in the Archives of American Agriculture at Iowa State University. He was praised for "his finest hour, namely, his courageous response to one of the worst crises in American history, the Dust Bowl and all its concomitant human misery and distress,"[31] and was said to have been "perhaps the only career civil servant without strong personal, social and political ties to create and lead a federal service."[32] Louis Bromfield credited him with:

> the old American virtues of integrity, simplicity, directness, and honor [...] I have seen, perhaps for the first time in history, a whole nation turning to right a wrong, to check an evil before it was forced to do so by utter disaster.[33]

The last edition of his book contained chapters on the various techniques of soil conservation practiced in his era: crop rotation, contouring, terracing, channels and outlets, gully control, control of stream banks, water spreading, farm ponds, stubble and mulch farming, farm drainage, farm irrigation, trees and shrubs, and upland flood control. He took the view that "40 to 50 million acres of land now cropped should be planted to trees, shrubs, grass and other adaptable plants." Noting that the CCC planted 257 million trees over a five-and-a-half-year period, he took the view that with adequate plant stock and plant technicians, the SCS could have planted ten times as much, and saw a need for planting 2 billion trees and shrubs annually over a 25-year period.[34]

The districts he established have been said to "provide an outlet for the energies of public-spirited farmers [...] opportunities are multiplied for many people to work off their aggressions and to fulfill their desires for a share in the organized power and influence in this country."[35] According to Brink,

> Hugh found it necessary to impress on his boys—and on everyone else, so far as he could—the necessity of keeping clear the independent identity of the districts. Repeatedly he would roar: "Watch it! They are not Soil Conservation *Service* districts!"[36]

In subsequent years, his agency's mission has become more diffused. It was renamed the Natural Resources Conservation Service in 1994; in the same year, a General Accounting Office report found a conflict between its mission to cooperate with farmers and the regulatory powers it had been given over conversion of wetlands.[37] Increasingly, with the growth of suburbs into un-zoned areas, the local committees became de facto land-use planning agencies.[38] A later article in *Government Executive* noted that "the farmer's helper has become a regulatory enforcer" and is "searching for the middle road";[39] in 1996, it was said to be "changing to meet the future."[40]

The 1985 law gave the SCS, as it then was, a role in enforcing environmental conditions on conservation subsidy payments; these conditions were aimed at air quality and wildlife habitat objectives not related to soil quality, generating sharp conflicts over inland wetlands; in addition the law was aimed at preventing "sod-busting" and "swamp-busting," rendering the SCS a so-called "green police." The 1985 law, the Food Security Act, also established a "conservation reserve" providing ten years of lease payments to farmers withdrawing their land from production, encompassing about 75,000 square miles. In 1990, a wetland reserve program was established, acquiring enough land to roughly offset the reduced level of wetland losses prevalent after the 1985 act. It was claimed that by 1982, "after 46 years and a $16 billion investment, no more than 25% to 35% of the nation's cropland is under approved conservation plans."[41] The 1985 law required plans for all affected areas by 1990 and full implementation of them by 1995; it was claimed that by 1996, erosion rates on about 250,000 square miles of designated highly erodible lands dropped from 17.4 tons per acre annually to 5.8 tons per acre, reducing the previous soil loss of 2.8 billion tons per year by a billion tons per year.[42] On the other hand, the program was highly expensive, costing about $1.8 billion per year to avoid 700 million tons of soil erosion. The program was directed heavily at water rather than wind erosion, even though wind erosion accounted for 880 million tons of soil a year, 44 percent of all erosion, and 80 percent of the erosion in Western states where rangeland was neglected.[43]

Developments in Canada, however, were well behind those in the United States. Canada achieved an 11 percent reduction in erosion in the period 1981–91, 5 percent from crop changes, and 6 percent from tilling changes; Ontario began an effective grass-roots program delivery mechanism, the Ontario Soil and Crop Improvement Association modeled on Bennett's Soil Conservation Districts, with a lag of nearly half a century.[44] Australia likewise stimulated grass-roots activity through a Landcare program that voluntarily enlisted 37 percent of Australia's farmers; it "succeeded beyond even the most optimistic of expectations" and was institutionalized in Land Conservation Districts in Western Australia, District Soil Boards in South Australia, Total Catchment Management Committees in New South Wales, and Catchment and Land Protection Boards in Victoria. The district concept was also embraced in South Africa and parts of Mexico.[45] The Australian approach included conversion of cropland to pasture, which generally reduces soil loss; low-density tree planting, which is less resisted by farmers than reforestation that withdraws land from production; and changes in water allocation policy to curb the "prior appropriation" doctrine and reduce irrigation. The program in Australia contemplates the planting of a billion trees in a decade: "The re-vegetation efforts are somewhat reminiscent of the Civilian Conservation Corps in the United States but one would hope that Landcare's tree planting will leave a longer legacy."[46]

In 1996, the US program had 9,400 federal employees in county offices and an additional 3,000 employees at the headquarters, a decline of about 1,500 employees since 1993. In addition there were 7,000 employees of districts on county payrolls, 16,500 district board members, 12,000 part-time volunteers, 800 state agency employees, and, a pale shadow of the CCC days, 550 Americorps workers. There were 2.3 million cooperating farm units and 1.7 million soil conservation plans. It was alleged that since 1985 new wetlands programs had established a no-net-loss situation with respect to wetlands with an 80 percent reduction in annual loss offset by reclamation programs, though in the preceding years there had been a 53 percent loss of wetlands to a level of 104 million acres, or about 160,000 square miles.[47]

The strategies used for wetlands included shallow dikes, drainage ditches, and blockage of subsurface drains, while those for highly erodible areas included greater use of crop residues and cover crops and grass on slopes.[48] While in 1996 it was claimed that the new rules had reduced soil erosion by 50 percent since 1985, and erosion from cropland by one-third,[49] their enforcement was unpopular with farmers, whose hostility resulted in SCS representatives no longer visiting farms alone. There was also a drastic change in the recruitment of SCS field personnel; until 1970, these were male graduates of agricultural colleges who were required to demonstrate that they had grown up on farms. After 1985, so-called "FSA [Farm Security Act] babies" were hired, frequently women with degrees in environmental science and wildlife ecology.[50] Agriculture by then accounted for 20 percent of employment in only one-fifth of America's counties; 28 percent of farms accounted for 86 percent of output. This constituted a realization of Bennett's prophecy that "farming will become an expert profession; the inexpert and inept will be forced off the land."[51] To avoid damage to local economies, the Conservation Reserve was limited to 25 percent of a county's land area. The new emphasis on riverbeds and steep slopes led to a hundred-fold increase in grassed waterways. The tying of farm subsidies to conservation plans gave rise to an increase in the client base of 20 percent. It was said that Bennett's "education-information-subsidy" policy became less effective over time; the policy of tying subsidies to conservation plans also became less effective as subsidies began to be phased out over a ten-year period under the 1966 Federal Agriculture Improvement and Reform Act; rising prices also made penalties less consequential.[52] By 2002, with the advent of the second Bush Administration, SCS and FSA, the related conservation set-aside program, had become big business, amounting to $2.8 billion in 2006; previously the program had operated under the political radar because "in the old days, the money wasn't big enough to matter."[53] Increased emphasis on water resources and pollution control meant that a higher percentage of appropriated funds was spent in the damper Eastern states. It was increasingly claimed that "command and control" policies were necessary to force use of expert applicators of insecticides and pesticides and use of costly "precision farming" techniques.[54] There were various proposals to consolidate FSA and NRCS and to federalize FSA's county employees, who were hired by locally chosen FSA districts; these proposals were driven by alleged conflicts of interest and the demands of civil rights organizations, but foundered in the face of district and farmer opposition: "[We] don't want people in Birckenstock sandals and silk shirts running their county offices."[55]

While the American farm population has sharply fallen, it is a source of strength for American agriculture that nearly one farmer in 50 serves on a board charged with responsibility for disseminating knowledge of conservation techniques. The example supplied by the NRCS has inspired the creation of similar institutions in Australia and Canada. While voluntary compliance with national purposes has its limits, institutions fostering it are at least the first necessary step to securing greater respect for environmental regulations in an increasingly crowded world.

If the NRCS has in some respects lost its way, there would seem to be scope still for a revived and intensified reforestation effort, including the planting of grasslands for both soil erosion and flood control purposes of the dimensions proposed by Bennett in the 1930s. Bennett's program fell victim to wartime labor shortages; the present rates of youth unemployment attest that these no longer exist. There may also be scope, both administrative and political, for creation of new outdoor recreation districts with dedicated funding sources. The experience of several large cities attests that foot and bicycle paths in suburban flood plains become wildly popular, though they are fostered now only by small private organizations like the Rails to Trails movement. No serious recent effort has been made to create a national network of youth hostels, though there are vestigial remnants of earlier endeavors. Although in recent years the national government under the Antiquities Act has on occasion set aside new areas for national parks in the public land Western states, few national parks have been created east of the Mississippi, although there would seem to be scope for their creation in states like Kentucky and West Virginia where there are already substantial national forests, and there is need for reforestation, land reclamation, and new sources of employment.

10

Byron Hanke and the Residential Community Association

The rise of the residential community association, a whole new level of government, is taken for granted by most Americans. It is today estimated that 68 million Americans in 28 million homes live under the jurisdiction of 338,000 residential community associations, which annually dispose of about $46 billion and have reserves of about $41 billion.[1] In 1991, residential community association budgets were greater than those of townships, about one-sixth those of counties, about one-tenth those of school districts, and about one-twelfth those of municipalities.[2] Some states provided for public enforcement of their covenants;[3] others required that they be notified of various proposed actions by public authority;[4] while others provided their residents with various tax dispensations in recognition of the associations' expenditures.[5] The person most responsible for this development is not an historic founder, like John Winthrop, John Locke or Thomas Jefferson, nor a nineteenth-century reformer like Joseph Pulitzer or William Leggett, but rather an obscure twentieth-century bureaucrat in what can only be described as a fourth-level bureaucratic position. Byron Hanke was not an elected official, nor a cabinet member, nor even an agency head. He was the Chief Land Planner for the Federal Housing Administration (FHA) from 1945 to 1972. He was born in 1911, took an undergraduate degree at Colgate, and trained as a landscape architect. He received a master's degree in landscape architecture at Harvard

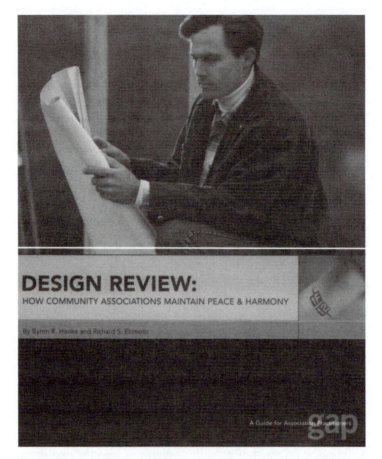

22. Byron Hanke, from *Design Review: How Community Associations Maintain Peace & Harmony* by Byron R. Hanke and Richard S. Ekimoto (Public domain)

in 1937, became the Charles Eliot Traveling Fellow in Europe in 1938, and received a second master's degree in urban planning in 1940. He was familiar with Ebenezer Howard's ideas and visited Radburn in this period. Thereafter, he worked briefly for the Tennessee Valley Authority before becoming a land planning consultant on wartime housing for the FHA in 1940 and Chief Land Planner in 1945.[6]

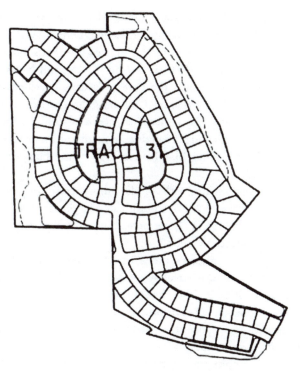

23. Example of a curvilinear development configuration. Courtesy of
Post, Buckley, Schuh, and Jernigan, Inc. Tampa, FL, 1992 (From *Land
Development for Civil Engineers*, Thomas R. Dion. Wiley, 2002)

Prior to his advent, there had been a few localized experiences
with homeowners' associations using deed covenants: the first was
that involving Louisburg Square in Boston in 1826, with covenants for upkeep being imposed by a homeowners' association
in 1844, then that in Gramercy Square in New York in 1831.
There had been an earlier development of the same type governing
Leicester Square in London in 1734, the covenants for which were
enforced in the famous Chancery case of *Tulk v. Moxhay* in 1848.[7]
In 1870, a Methodist camp meeting on similar lines had been
established at Ocean Grove in New Jersey (the strictness of whose
regulations caused it to be later referred to as "the grove of Sunday

silence"). In 1871, there was a similar development at Squirrel Island in Maine. The first large-scale development was that of Roland Park in Baltimore in 1891, followed by other subdivisions in the city: Guilford (1912), Homeland (1924), and Northwood (1932). There then ensued the Forest Gardens development in Queens, New York in 1913, the Country Club District in Kansas City in 1914, Sunnyside Gardens in Queens in 1924, Radburn in New Jersey in 1929, and a small development known as Scientist's Cliffs in Calvert County, Maryland in 1937, where Hanke bought a lot in 1949.[8]

Later developments with similar idiosyncratic origins were Irvine, California (1971), Columbia, Maryland (1967), and Reston, Virginia (1965). There were about 500 community associations in existence by 1962.[9]

Hanke, in his master's thesis in 1937, had urged developments with curvilinear street systems, neighborhood parks, and recreation facilities. In 1941, he contributed several chapters to an influential book on subdivision regulations, including a chapter on dedicated open space that cited the examples of the Country Club District and Radburn.[10]

In 1952, Hanke and Andre Faure of the FHA wrote a booklet on *Suggested Land Subdivision Regulations*, reprinted in 1959, 1960, and 1962.[11] This included an outline of model covenants, but did not include provision for charges and for a community association. This had much to do with the layout of postwar American suburbs, with their repudiation of grid street patterns and their use of undulating roads. It included as a suggestion:

> In developments where adequate public maintenance of park areas, streets or other facilities is not available, it is advisable to establish a property owners' maintenance association with adequate powers to provide maintenance and to assess the benefiting property owners at a reasonable rate and collect such assessments.[12]

Modifications to the National Housing Act extended FHA insurance coverage to cooperatives in 1950 and to condominiums in 1961; in 1955, Congress provided the FHA commissioner with a special assistant for cooperative housing.[13]

Cooperative housing was largely confined, then as now, to New York City, and usually was the product of private agreements outside a statutory framework. Condominium housing, in which each apartment owner had deeded ownership of record, not merely a lease and shares of stock, is said to have been referred to in the Napoleonic Code of 1804 as "co-proprietare." It received statutory recognition in Brazil in 1928, in Chile in 1937, and in most Latin American countries in the 1940s and 1950s, followed by Mexico in 1967–8. Its use in Puerto Rico was recognized in section 234 of the National Housing Act of 1961. By mid-1968, the FHA had insured 1,163 condominiums for a total of $21.7 million; of these, 818 units totaling $16.6 million were in Puerto Rico, the others being in California, the District of Columbia, Florida, and Michigan.[14]

In December 1963, Hanke, after spending time as a federal executive fellow at the Brookings Institution, organized a study of cluster housing and common property ownership at the Urban Land Institute, for which he secured funds from the FHA, the National Association of Home Builders, and four other federal agencies. The resulting 64-page study was released in December 1963 at the annual convention of the National Association of Home Builders.[15] More than 50,000 copies of this document were distributed.[16]

The brochure described the requirements for qualifying for FHA insurance where cluster development was resorted to. It revealed that there might be higher initial costs, but greater appeal to buyers. FHA insurance standards were modified to allow greater flexibility in land planning, through use of a new concept of "land use intensity" to measure density,[17] which "automatically provides open space in an amount related to total floor space or number of people."[18] It required that all cluster developments have an automatic-membership homes association holding the common property, with association charges as liens and lot owner voting rights to ensure that the community association could survive separately from the developer.

Hanke's insight was the same as that elsewhere expressed by the legal scholar Carol Rose:

In the absence of the socializing activities that take place on "inherently public property," the public is a shapeless mob, whose members neither trade nor converse nor play, but only fight, in a setting where life is, in Hobbes' all too famous phrase, solitary, poor, nasty, brutish and short.[19]

The FHA and Urban Land Institute thereafter published, as Urban Land Institute Technical Bulletin 50, a *Homes Association Handbook* of 422 pages.[20] The bulletin urged that associations be formed quickly and assume responsibilities early, to give residents experience in administration. The book anticipated virtually all the problems that arise in the operations of homeowners' associations, and has been aptly described as "part marketing research, part legal analysis, part architectural design, and part organizational theory."[21] What it produced was "a consumer product sold by a profit-making firm, a legal device, a corporation reliant on both coercive powers and voluntary cooperation, a philosophy, a democracy, and a lifestyle."[22] It was later said that:

This book has had a greater impact on the land use patterns of American cities than any other book in our nation's history. It told how and why the patterns established by the traditional residential subdivision could be improved upon by clustering housing in planned unit developments. It triggered a change in the way of life of hundreds of communities and home builders.[23]

In the words of Robert Nelson: "If RCAs [residential community associations] were to become the prevailing mode of social organization for the local community, this development could be as important as the adoption of the private corporate form for business property."[24]

Residential community associations were of a size that was viewed as almost ideal for community life by myriad political theorists and social scientists. Thus, for example, Rousseau, in chapter 4 of his Social Contract, wrote:

In the first place the state must be sufficiently small to make it possible to call the whole people together without difficulty and each citizen must be in a position to know all his neighbors. In the second place, manners must be so simple that business will be kept to a minimum and thorny questions avoided. There should be too considerable equality in fortune and rank, for otherwise there will not long be equality in rights and authority. Finally, there must be little or no luxury, because [...] it corrupts both the rich and the poor, the rich through their possessions, the poor through their lust to possess.

Among the functions for which residential community associations may possess a competitive advantage are street cleaning, refuse collection, street paving, janitorial service, and traffic signal and swimming pool maintenance, as well as day-care and elder-care, demand–response transportation, cooperative purchasing, neighborhood watch, and the operation of health clinics and chartering of convenience stores. They have the capacity to integrate the services of volunteers and paid workers. They may properly be given a role in reviewing land-use applications. Early cases barring requirements that neighbors consent have been supplanted by cases allowing local referenda.[25] Neighbors are entitled to some assurance that the status quo in land use will continue.

A variety of technical bulletins were later published. In November 1971, Hanke wrote *A Proposal for a National Council of Homes Associations*, which became a reality in 1973; it now has 30,000 members. In 1976, while at the Community Associations Institute (CAI) after his retirement, he published *Creating a Community Association: The Developer's Role in Community and Homeowner Associations*. He envisioned CAI as a research and education institute with three classes of members: homeowners, associations, and developers. Under CAI's constitution, concurrence of representatives of each group was requisite to the taking of a formal position. Later, he wrote a short pamphlet designed to minimize highly publicized conflicts between owners and the community association arising from design review covenants.[26]

In 1964, during the Nixon Administration, the FHA with Hanke's guidance began to promote a program known as CHOICE, an acronym for Cost Effective Home Ownership and Improved Contemporary Environment. The program included townhouses on 2,500-square-foot lots with 32 acres of open space, designed to sell for about two-thirds the median home price. In Hanke's words: "HUD Secretary George Romney folded the CHOICE program into his Operation Breakthrough to help his ill-fated program for manufactured housing." In the early 1980s, the scheme was revived under Housing and Urban Development Secretary Jack Kemp as a Housing Cost Reduction Demonstration.

The acceptance of residential community associations was such that municipalities as well as the FHA began to require that all new developments have residential community associations.[27] Puerto Rico, a densely populated territory with many apartment-dwellers, had introduced the condominium device familiar in a number of Latin American countries. Developers of Puerto Rican condominiums sought federal mortgage insurance, and in 1961, section 234 of the National Housing Act made mortgage insurance available to Puerto Rican condominiums; in 1964 the act was further amended to eliminate any requirement that the developer first have been insured under another program. By 1968, federal mortgage insurance had been extended to about 400 condominium projects in Puerto Rico, the District of Columbia, and three states—California, Florida, and Michigan—which had followed Puerto Rico in enacting condominium acts. The FHA in 1961 distributed model condominium legislation, variants of which were adopted in all 50 states by 1967.[28] By 1987 there were 4.2 million units of condominium housing in the United States. Time-sharing of condominiums, which began in Ticino, Switzerland in 1963 and in Hawaii in 1968, is also a widely authorized and practiced phenomenon; by 1999, there were 1,608 timeshare developments in the United States and 5,156 worldwide, with 4.5 million owners worldwide.[29] The British authorized condominium housing by enactment of the Commonhold and Leasehold Reform Act, chapter 15 of the Acts of 2002, the first creation of a new property interest since 1925, though the device has since been little used in Britain.

The FHA was concerned with the burden cast on municipalities by decaying infrastructure in cheaply built tract developments. Its interest in community associations had been stimulated by Hanke, a man who exerted a major influence on the shape of suburban America. In 1941, as shown by Donald Stabile,[30] he contributed to a study of subdivision regulations promoting the use of curvilinear streets and park areas. In 1959, he prepared an FHA booklet on subdivision regulations suggesting in passing the use of community associations with assessment powers to maintain park areas.

In 1963, as previously noted, the FHA published a handbook, *Planned Unit Development With a Home Association*, requiring that developers of planned-unit developments establish homeowners' associations with assessment powers by deed covenants: "There are certain legal musts which FHA requires in connection with an agency approval of a planned unit development. The [documents] must legally create an automatic-membership nonprofit homes association [and] place an association charge on each lot." The authority for this sort of requirement was conferred by section 203(c) of the National Housing Act of 1934: "no mortgage shall be accepted for insurance [...] unless the Administrator finds that the project with respect to which the mortgage is executed is economically sound." In the words of Evan McKenzie:

> Forty to fifty thousand copies of the publication were circulated, and it was a major factor in the PUD boom that followed [...] [T]he document was distributed at the NAHB [National Association of Home Builders] meeting. Its impact was enormous [...] "The industry grabbed the idea, and local government accepted it, and FHA insured it, and the concept took off like wildfire."[31]

In 1964, the Urban Land Institute published a 422-page *Homes Association Handbook* edited by Hanke, 10,000 copies of which were distributed over the ensuing ten years. The work was described by a former president of the Urban Land Institute as having "had a greater impact on the land use patterns of American cities than any other book in our nation's history."[32] Shortly thereafter, organization of such associations was required in order for lenders on new developments to obtain federal mortgage insurance. By 1988, there were 130,000 residential community and condominium associations covering some 29 million people, about 12 percent of the population.[33] In 1998, there were 205,000 associations with 42 million residents, about 15 percent of the population. By 2015, there were more than 338,000 associations with 27 million homes and 68 million residents, 20 percent of the population. Roughly half of new construction is in associations. In some rapidly growing portions of Southern California, 70 percent of the population lived under the jurisdiction of a residential community association.[34] Some 55 percent of the associations governed condominiums, 15 percent of them governed detached tract housing, and 39 percent governed townhouse developments. The average association fee in 2010 was $867 annually, the median fee $336. Some 94 percent of the associations maintained outdoor areas, 72 percent undertook trash collection, 67 percent maintained swimming pools, and 31 percent maintained security patrols.

The associations have many advantages as providers of services. They are small enough to be able to enlist the volunteer labor of their members, to engage in what public administration scholars call "co-production" of services. They have no bureaucracies of their own, and thus have no conflicts of interest when they contract for services with third parties; they are "pure provision units." They thus can contract out services like road repair and trash collection and acquire such services much more cheaply than municipalities with their unionized workforces. Increasingly, in recognition of this, municipalities are according them credits against property taxes for services thus assumed; there are statutes in Montgomery County, Maryland[35] and in New Jersey requiring such credits. While dues paid to these private associations are not tax deductible, that limitation is increasingly being circumvented through the incorporation of parallel taxing districts with the same land area to render services that are municipal in character and which therefore attract tax deductibility; this device is widely employed in Anne Arundel County, Maryland and in some places in Pennsylvania and Connecticut. Increasingly, such private associations are being accorded the power to waive public zoning restrictions; more than a dozen states have authorized associations to waive zoning-imposed prohibitions of day-care centers.

A new model covenant published by Wayne Hyatt of Atlanta, perhaps the nation's leading practitioner of community association law, would expressly allow associations to render various social services such as day-care and demand–response transportation, provided the services are financed with user charges. The Uniform Common Interests Act (UCIA) promulgated by the National Conference of Commissioners on Uniform Laws has been amended to allow 80 percent of residents to modify use restrictions or impose new restrictions, provided that they are not applied to current unit owners; the amended model covenants also allow landlords to agree in a lease to give a tenant voting rights. Typically, a super-majority of all residents is needed for major changes, such as special assessments; because many associations are located in vacation areas,[36] the UCIA imposes only a 20 percent quorum requirement for meetings.[37]

The American Law Institute's *Restatement of Servitudes* contains provisions designed to discourage litigation by making resort to alternative dispute resolution mandatory. Problems of corruption have been avoided by the provision in state condominium and residential association laws of provisions rendering annual private audits mandatory. A private organization known as the Community Associations Institute, with 17,000 members and a staff of 45 by 1999, offers training courses and publishes manuals of good practice. It was organized in the early 1970s with the encouragement of the late Elliot Richardson, then Secretary of Housing and Urban Development.

By giving suburban residents a sense of control over their immediate environment and maintaining infrastructure, the associations have done much to maintain their residents' satisfaction with suburban life, and to avoid the creation of feelings of alienation that would otherwise have been directed at frequently remote town and county governments. Regrettably, the organization of school districts in most places precludes the associations being given a formal role in governing the local elementary school and lending support to it. In Britain, by contrast, the lowest level of government, the parish council, may elect a member of the board of governors of the nearest elementary school.[38]

A critic of community associations, Evan McKenzie, has lamented the fact that "the role of government has been largely permissive and promotional rather than regulatory or directive."[39] That is the secret of the success of the concept. The government's efforts to construct new communities, both during the New Deal and in connection with the Johnson Administration's Model Cities program, foundered on lack of management flexibility and disregard of consumer preferences. Only three small towns, each with fewer than 1,000 units, were built during the New Deal; they became upper-middle-class developments because of cost over-runs. Twelve of the 13 Model Cities developments with 250,000 projected units ran out of money, the program ultimately costing the government $561 million.[40] The 300,000 community associations have nearly 2 million board members enjoying significant rights of civic participation and thereby gaining greater understanding of appropriate political behavior. In many large suburban counties with remote county governments and few municipalities (Baltimore County, Maryland, for example), there would be far more political and social alienation but for Byron Hanke's social inventions.

The FHA and the federal mortgage guarantee institutions have fallen into the hands of unconstructive bureaucrats, some of them seriously corrupt. Hanke's guides to development and required development conditions have gone unmodified, even though ample scope exists for modifications, which would involve no innovations in principle. The width of required collector roads can be decreased to reflect the demise of the gas-guzzler era; regulations of required curbs and lighting can be relaxed. More important, the inclusion in at least larger new developments of such amenities as accessory apartments, very small convenience stores in residences,[41] old age clubs, pre-school playgroups, charter schools, and zip cars or other forms of demand–response transportation can be usefully considered to accommodate recent dramatic changes in demography and family structure.[42] The FHA no longer has the potential influence it once did when it insured the lion's share of residential mortgages; that share fell to only 3 percent in 2006, though under the impact of the foreclosure crisis it rose to 40 percent in 2012.

CONCLUSION: THE WAY FORWARD

I t is easy to catalog the flaws of much recent legislation, with its over-regulation dampening individual and local initiative; its perverse incentives, moral hazards, and unintended consequences; its assumption that good intentions produce good results; its too-frequent refusal to legislate for people as they are. "The construction of a theoretical paradise is the easiest of human efforts," Charles Evans Hughes observed. "This is a far lighter undertaking than the necessary and unspectacular task, taking human nature as it is and is likely to remain, of contriving improvements that are workable."[1] The premise of what follows is that what most people still want is the modest utopia described by Michael J. Bennett in his book on the GI Bill: "living in a system that rewards being an honest citizen and a hard worker."[2] There are here tendered some suggestions whose practicability has been demonstrated and that accord with that premise:

1. The national government can no longer foster state, local, and private initiative through grants of land, but the successor to the public domain is the command of public finance deriving from the 16th Amendment and the income tax. It is neither legitimate nor efficient for the national government to attempt to regulate all local and private activity through the device of conditional grants in aid. The national legislatures of all the major countries of Western Europe: Germany, France, Britain, Italy, and Spain have in the last 40 years found it possible to accord provincial and/or local governments guaranteed shares of the national income tax.[3] It is time for the United States to follow suit.[4] Not only does the income tax grow more rapidly

than local revenue sources, but inflation bears more heavily on labor-intensive local governments than on national governments whose expenditures are weighted toward transfers or purchase of manufactured products benefiting from productivity gains. The consequence of such tax-sharing would almost certainly be a somewhat larger public sector, by reason of the principle of public finance economics summarized as "money sticks where it hits." That fact may make the change acceptable to at least some of the federal government's client groups, and provides a fair trade-off for the disappearance of suffocating controls.

2. State and local business tax structures are increasingly outmoded, complicated, and perverse. Taxes on profits and personal property burden manufacturers, who must retain earnings to improve plant, and fall lightly on service industries. Wider adoption of income VATs, like the rather simple Business Enterprise Tax in New Hampshire,[5] would alleviate this problem. These taxes are broad-based, and fall without exemption on payroll, dividends, and retained profits. Their adoption would not only be a simplifying measure, but would benefit cities into which workers commute if used as a basis of local taxation or state-shared taxes.

3. The mediocrity of our public schools, bound hand and foot by recruitment and compensation rules imposed by unions, has been recognized since the 1950s. The only cures being pressed are vouchers and charter schools, which involve not reform of what already exists but erection of entire new systems. Despite 20 years of controversy, the new panaceas account for barely 1 percent of high school enrollment. Britain, Australia, New Zealand, Denmark, Switzerland, and several German *Länder* have effectively made all schools charter schools, by giving each its building-level board.

4. Various writers, including Robert Ellickson and Robert Nelson, have pointed to the need for "new institutions for old neighborhoods" by allowing voluntary organization of associations

at the election precinct level, with limited assessment powers and the authority to construct improvements and organize services like day-care and local transportation. French communes and to a lesser extent British parish councils with typical populations of fewer than 1,000 provide such services.

5. The Japanese, with modest tax credits, have fostered the creation of old-age clubs, realizing that at any given time most elders are not bed-ridden and welcome useful activity. These mutual aid organizations provide many social services.[6] Several nations provide incentives to mutual aid among extended families by stimulating the creation of duplex, accessory, or "mother-in-law" apartments in single-family housing.

6. Grandiose reform proposals for health care have insured that many Americans have no health coverage at all. The prejudice against socialized medicine has resulted in neglect of Peter Drucker's assessment of the voucher system for primary care in the British National Health Service: "The part that pays physicians for patients on their lists works extremely well [...] For standard medical care, government in the National Health Service is an insurance company. It reimburses the doctor who takes care of a patient. But the doctor does not become a government employee. Nor is the patient in any way limited as to what doctor to choose."[7] British primary care physicians, at least until recently, enjoyed more clinical freedom than their American counterparts, who must answer to multiple insurers with different practices and rules.

7. Several nations have developed a method of urban renewal known as "land readjustment."[8] Owners on a city block vote to cooperatively redevelop the block. Dissenting owner-occupiers are excused. Other dissenters, upon approval, have a right to be bought out at appraised value. The remaining owners organize, allocate shares by value, and award shares to a developer, usually the promoter of the plan. This avoids the delays of land acquisition, and is adaptable to inner-city slums. More than half the war-damaged real estate in Japan was restored

using this device, which exploits the profit motive rather than running counter to it.

8. Except for housing, American society in its lower reaches is not Disraeli's "property-owning democracy." Savings rates are low, and the Bush scheme for partial privatization of social security and the Gore scheme for government matching of savings have disappeared in the manner of election-year gambits. Melding these approaches seems possible, and the success of ambitious "forced savings" schemes like that of Singapore suggests that modestly increased payroll taxation is politically acceptable if greater personal autonomy and security results.[9]

9. The much-vexed problem of illegal immigration may also yield to solutions based on the traditional American preference for the association of benefits and obligations, federalism, and local control. One can conceive of a regime in which millions of law-abiding illegal immigrants who have successfully established themselves in the United States are granted resident alien status on condition that they, their friends, family, or employers pay a substantial application fee or civil penalty, perhaps of $5,000 per person. The billions of dollars thus raised might be earmarked for programs designed to address illegal immigration at its source, by improving public health services and the availability of nurse practitioners in the Central American countries with abnormally high birth rates and by expanding the Merida program for police training there. In addition, the nation's dormant local Selective Service boards, consisting of thousands of respected local civic volunteers, might be employed to assist in the vetting of applicants for permits and the organization of settlement houses and language classes; such bodies inspire more confidence than the Washington-based Immigration and Naturalization Service. Finally, the much-vexed problem of suffrage and the attendant demands for "paths to citizenship" could be left to the states, as Article I, Sections 2 and 4 of the Constitution contemplates. Prior to the early 1920s, nearly two dozen states enfranchised resident aliens, their actions in doing so being effective for both

state and federal elections; women's suffrage spread gradually through the states for 50 years (and may have been decisive in the 1916 presidential election) prior to the adoption of the 19th Amendment in 1920.

10. A similar notion of reciprocity of obligation underlaid the youth employment programs of the New Deal, most notably the Civilian Conservation Corps, organized by General George Marshall, in which millions of young men received work-readiness training in exchange for unskilled or semi-skilled labor on projects of a type that are still needed: soil conservation, flood control, reforestation, land reclamation, and the creation of new national parks and trails. Workers under the age of 25 might be excused from payroll taxation, a uniform and self-executing measure that would be far less expensive than the 2 percent across-the-board payroll tax holiday temporarily enacted by the Obama Administration as an economic stimulus measure, and younger workers might also be given access to the United States Employment Service, now an almost moribund agency available only to recipients of unemployment insurance.

The unifying themes of these proposals are devolution, reciprocity of obligations, institution-building, and predictability. They are designed to supplant central government mandates, funded and unfounded; the almost incomprehensible recent federal education bill is the *reductio ad absurdum* of that approach. The view taken here is that of Tocqueville:

Sometimes the centralized power, in its despair, invokes the assistance of the citizens; it says to them: "You shall act just as I please, as much as I please, and in the direction which I please. You are to take charge of the details, without aspiring to guide the system; you are to work in darkness; and afterwards you may judge my work by its results." These are not the conditions upon which the alliance of the human will is to be obtained; it must be free in its style, and responsible for its acts, or (such is the constitution of man) the citizen had rather remain a passive spectator, than a dependent actor, in schemes with which he is unacquainted.[10]

Some of our proposals, to be sure, involve the use of state power, like all our benign examples. We have shown that the "conservatives" in Congress and elsewhere who believe that all beneficial activity is private misread the lessons of our history. In James Willard Hurst's words: "Not the jealous limitation of the power of the state but the release of individual creative energy was the dominant value";[11] the ten subjects of our essays provide examples of how enlightened draftsmen can empower citizens. As Nelson posits: "If neighborhoods are to become more important, new legal mechanisms are necessary to provide the requisite institutional support and foundation."[12] According to Wiebe:

> What the democrat asks is that just as few as possible of [...] rights be sealed apart from political life, just as many as possible embedded in a majoritarian process. The rights themselves depend upon it. As recent events have demonstrated, those champions of individual rights who live by the judiciary die by the judiciary.[13]

NOTES

Introduction

1 E.g. Antiterrorism and Effective Death Penalty Act of 1996, Public Law 104–32.
2 *U.S. v. Oakland Cannabis Buyers' Cooperative*, 532 U.S. 483, at n.9 (2001).
3 *Gonzales v. Raich*, 545 U.S. 1 (2005).
4 *Brooklyn Natl, Corp. v. C.I.R.*, 157 F. 2d 450, 451 (2nd Cir., 1946).
5 R. Wiebe, *Self Rule: A Cultural History of American Democracy* (Chicago: University of Chicago Press, 1995), 207.
6 T. Lowi, *The End of Liberalism* (New York: Norton, 2nd edn., 1977), 63.
7 Ibid., xii.

1. John Locke and Southern Plantations

1 J. Aronson, "Shaftesbury on Locke," 53 *American Political Science Review* 1103 (1959).
2 The text referred to here is that in D. Wooton (ed.), *John Locke: Political Writings* (Harmondsworth: Penguin, 1993), 210–32. This corresponds to the 1670 version in M. Parker (ed.), *North Carolina Charters and Constitutions, 1578–1698* (Raleigh, NC: Carolina Charter Tercentenary Commission, 1963), 165–85.
3 Sir Peter Colleton to Locke, October 1673, in E. De Beer (ed.), *The Correspondence of John Locke* (Oxford: Clarendon Press, 1976), vol. I, No. 279, 395.
4 D. Defoe, "Party-Tyranny" (1705), in A. Salley, *Narratives of Early Carolina, 1650–1708* (New York: Scribner's, 1911), 232.
5 J. Milton, "John Locke and the Fundamental Constitutions of Carolina," 21 *Locke Newsletter* 111 (1990).
6 Voltaire, *Traite de la Tolerance* (1763) (J. Renwick, ed.) (Oxford: Voltaire Foundation, 2000), 152.

7 P. Des Meizeaux (ed.), *A Collection of Several Pieces of Mr. John Locke* (London: R. Francklin, 1st edn., 1720; 2nd edn., 1739). A copy of the second edition is in the Library of King's College, Cambridge.

8 P. Laslett, "John Locke, the Great Recoinage, and the Origins of the Board of Trade, 1695–1698," in R. Ashcraft (ed.), *John Locke: Critical Assessments* (London: Routledge, 1991), vol. I, 181. See also M. Duff, "Creating a Plantation Province," and G. Hewitt, "The State in the Planters' Service," in J. Greene, R. Brana-Shute, and R. Sparks (eds), *Money, Trade and Power: The Evolution of Colonial South Carolina's Plantation Society* (Columbia, SC: University of South Carolina Press, 2001).

9 N. Wood, *John Locke and Agrarian Capitalism* (Berkeley, CA: University of California Press, 1984), 22.

10 M. Cranston, *John Locke: A Biography* (London: Longmans, 1957), 120.

11 B. Arneil, *John Locke and America: The Defence of British Colonialism* (Oxford: Clarendon, 1996), 69.

12 M. Goldie, "Locke and America," in M. Stuart (ed.), *A Companion to Locke* (Oxford: Blackwell, 2016), 549.

13 Cranston, *John Locke*, 120 and n.3.

14 Arneil, *John Locke and America*, 3.

15 Ibid., 68–9.

16 J. Farr, "Locke, Natural Law, and New World Slavery," 36 *Political Theory* 495 (2008).

17 Cranston, *John Locke*, 419.

18 C. McGuinness, "The Fundamental Constitutions of Carolina as a Tool for Lockean Scholarship," 17 *Interpretation* 127 (1989).

19 Ibid., 107.

20 Arneil, *John Locke and America*, 10.

21 Cranston, *John Locke*, 419.

22 Arneil, *John Locke and America*, 18.

23 Ibid.

24 Ibid., 127.

25 J. Farr, "'So Vile and Miserable an Estate': The Problem of Slavery in Locke's Political Thought," 14 *Political Theory* 263 (1986).

26 G. Hill (ed.), *Boswell's Life of Johnson* (Oxford: Oxford University Press, 1934), vol. II, 201, quoted in Farr, "So Vile and Miserable an Estate," 263.

27 J. Bentham, *Papers* (Edinburgh: W. Tait, 1843), vol. IV, 432–3, quoted in D. Armitage, "John Locke, Carolina, and the Two Treatises of Government," 32 *Political Theory* 602 (2004).

28 J. Waldron, *God, Locke and Equality: Christian Foundations of John Locke's Political Thought* (Cambridge: Cambridge University Press, 2002), 206.

29 R. Middleton and A. Lombard, *Colonial America: A History to 1763* (Oxford: Wiley-Blackwell, 4th edn., 2011), 151.

30 B. Brownell and D. Goldfield (eds), *The City in Southern History* (Port Washington, NY: Kennikat Press, 1977), 23.

31 Armitage, "John Locke, Carolina"; see also J. Farr, "The Problem of Slavery in Locke's Political Thought," 14 *Political Theory* 263 (1986); Waldron, *God, Locke and Equality*, 197–206.

32 M. Seliger, *The Liberal Politics of John Locke* (London: Allen & Unwin, 1968), 278–83.

33 E. Sirmans, *Colonial South Carolina: A Political History 1663–1763* (Chapel Hill, NC: University of North California Press, 1966), 12ff.

34 J. Murrin, "Political Development," in J. Greene (ed.), *Colonial British America: Essays in the New History of the Early Modern Era* (Baltimore, MD: Johns Hopkins University Press, 1984), 419.

35 Armitage, "John Locke, Carolina."

36 D. Wooton, "John Locke and Richard Ashcraft's Revolutionary Politics," 40 *Political Studies* 79 (1992), quoted in Wooton (ed.), *John Locke: Political Writings*, 44.

37 The 1682 version is reproduced in University Microfilms, L2744, English Books 1641–1700.

38 R. Waterhouse, *A New World Gentry: The Making of a Merchant and Planter Class in South Carolina, 1670–1730* (New York: Garland, 1989), 29–30.

39 Ibid., 29.

40 V. Hsueh, "Giving Orders: Theory and Practice in the Fundamental Constitution of Carolina," 63 *Journal of the History of Ideas* 425, 436, 438 (2002).

41 C. Andrews, *The Colonial Period of American History* (New Haven, CT: Yale University Press, 1937), vol. III, 182ff.

42 D. Galenson, "The Settlement and Growth of the Colonies: Population, Labor, and Economic Development," in S. Engerman and R. Gallman (eds), *The Cambridge Economic History of the United States, Vol. I: The Colonial Era* (Cambridge: Cambridge University Press, 1996), 145.

43 Murrin, "Political Development," 418.

44 Ibid., 413.

45 Galenson, "Settlement and Growth of the Colonies," 145.

46 Ibid., 144.

47 Ibid., 146.

48 Waterhouse, *A New World Gentry*, 30ff.

49 Sirmans, *Colonial South Carolina*, 60.

50 J. Hagy, *This Happy Land: The Jews of Colonial and Antebellum Charleston* (Tuscaloosa, AL: University of Alabama Press, 1993), 1.

51 Defoe, "Party-Tyranny," 238 (editor's note).

52 Andrews, *The Colonial Period of American History*, 216, n.3.

53 Hagy, *This Happy Land*, 28–35.

54 Andrews, *The Colonial Period of American History*, 182ff.

55 W. Craven, *The Southern Colonies in the Seventeenth Century, 1607–1689* (Baton Rouge, LA: Louisiana State University Press, 1949), 345.
56 See generally W. Edgar, *South Carolina: A History* (Columbia, SC: University of South Carolina Press, 1998).
57 P. Gates, *History of Public Land Law Development* (Washington, DC: GPO, 1978), 35.
58 *Second Treatise on Government*, sec. 45; see also *Letter Concerning Toleration* (1685).
59 Sirmans, *Colonial South Carolina*, 60.
60 Gates, *History of Public Land Law Development*, 36.
61 Parker, *North Carolina Charters and Constitutions*, 234–40.
62 J. Daniels, *Tar Heels: A Portrait of North Carolina* (New York: Dodd Mead, 1941), 338.
63 R. Sheridan, "The Domestic Economy," in Greene (ed.), *Colonial British America*, 53–4.
64 Murrin, "Political Development," 444.
65 Sirmans, *Colonial South Carolina*, 12ff.
66 Murrin, "Political Development."
67 Middleton and Lombard, *Colonial America*, 222.
68 S. Sarson, *British America 1500–1800: Creating Colonies, Imagining an Empire* (London: Hodder, 2005), 126.
69 C. Graham, *The South Carolina State Constitution* (New York: Oxford University Press, 2011).
70 Ibid., 15.
71 D. Hawke, *The Colonial Experience* (Indianapolis: Bobbs-Merrill, 1966), 214.
72 Middleton and Lombard, *Colonial America*, 222; R. Jennings, *The Creation of America: Through Revolution to Empire* (Cambridge: Cambridge University Press, 2000), 44.
73 J. Bryce, *American Commonwealth* (New York: Macmillan, 1895), vol. I, 591–2.
74 Sirmans, *Colonial South Carolina*, 60ff.
75 Ibid., 10, 14.
76 Waterhouse, *A New World Gentry*, 109.
77 A. De Tocqueville, *Democracy in America* (H. Mansfield and D. Winthrop, trans.) (Chicago: University of Chicago Press, 2000), 313, 334.
78 Ibid., 343, 348.
79 Graham, *The South Carolina State Constitution*, 20, 26.
80 Ibid., 84.
81 Jennings, *The Creation of America*, 33.
82 Ibid., 45.
83 R. Wiebe, *Self Rule: A Cultural History of American Democracy* (Chicago: University of Chicago Press, 1995), 139.

84 Graham, *The South Carolina State Constitution*, 9–11.
85 P. Drucker, *The End of Economic Man: A Study of the New Totalitarianism* (New Brunswick, NJ: Transaction Books, 1939).
86 S. Weil, *The Need for Roots: Prelude to a Declaration of Duties towards Mankind* (London: Routledge, 1952).

2. John Winthrop and the New England Town

1 O. Handlin, "Preface," in E. Morgan, *The Puritan Dilemma: The Story of John Winthrop* (Boston: Little Brown, 1958).
2 J. Winthrop, "Common Grievances Groaning for Reformation" (1623–4), in Massachusetts Historical Society, *Winthrop Papers* (Boston, 1929), vol. I, 268 [hereafter *Winthrop Papers*], quoted in D. Rutman, *Winthrop's Boston: Portrait of a Puritan Town* (Chapel Hill, NC: University of North California Press, 1965), 6.
3 *Winthrop Papers*, I, 373.
4 Ibid., I, 418.
5 Ibid., II, 151.
6 Morgan, *The Puritan Dilemma*, 8.
7 *Winthrop Papers*, II, 231.
8 S. Morison, *Builders of the Bay Colony* (Oxford: Oxford University Press, 1930), vi.
9 P. Smith, *As a City upon a Hill: The Town in American History* (New York: Knopf, 1966), 111.
10 Morison, *Builders of the Bay Colony*, 58.
11 V. Parrington, *The Colonial Mind, 1620–1800* (New York: Harcourt Brace, 1927), 47.
12 R. Dunn and L. Yeandle (eds), *The Journal of John Winthrop* (Cambridge, MA: Belknap Press, 1996), 1–11.
13 Smith, *As a City upon a Hill*, 13.
14 A. Taylor, *American Colonies: The Settling of North America* (New York: Penguin, 2001), 165, 170, 186.
15 P. Johnson, "Preface," in D. Beito, P. Gordon, A. Tabarrok, and Centre for Civil Society (eds), *The Voluntary City: Markets, Communities, and Urban Planning* (New Delhi: Academic Foundation, 2002), 14.
16 *Winthrop Papers*, III, 181.
17 C. Adrian and E. Griffith, *A History of American City Government, Vol. I: The Colonial Period* (New York: Oxford University Press, 1938), 34.
18 Winthrop Papers, III, 223.
19 A. De Tocqueville, *Democracy in America* (H. Mansfield and D. Winthrop, trans.) (Chicago: University of Chicago Press, 2000), 76.
20 Ibid., 150.
21 G. Haskins, *Law and Authority in Early Massachusetts* (New York: Macmillan, 1960), 29, 220.

22 F. Bremer, *John Winthrop: America's Forgotten Founding Father* (New York: Oxford University Press, 2003), 218, 241.

23 Quoted in ibid., 245.

24 J. Sly, *Town Government in Massachusetts (1620–1930)* (Cambridge, MA: Harvard University Press, 1935), 5ff.

25 E. Morgan, *The Founding of Massachusetts: Historians and the Sources* (New York: Bobbs-Merrill, 1964), 127.

26 Morison, *Builders of the Bay Colony*, 97.

27 F. Bremer, "The County of Massachusetts: The Governance of John Winthrop's Suffolk and the Shaping of the Massachusetts Bay Colony," in F. Bremer and L. Botelho, *The World of John Winthrop* (Charlottesville, VA: University of Virginia Press, 2005), 187, 208–36.

28 Haskins, *Law and Authority*, 130.

29 Quoted, with archaisms eliminated, in ibid., 129. See also C. Hilkey, *Legal Development in Colonial Massachusetts, 1630–86* (New York: Columbia University Press, 1910).

30 F. Bremer, *John Winthrop: Biography as History* (New York: Continuum, 2009), 30.

31 See A. Eaton, "Origins of Municipal Incorporation in England and in the United States," Proceedings of the American Bar Association, August 1902. See also A. Eaton, *Constitution Making in Rhode Island* (Providence, RI: Rhode Island Constitutional League, 1899).

32 207 U.S. 161 (1907). *Accord, Commonwealth v. Plaisted*, 148 Mass. 375 (1889).

33 Eaton, "Origins of Municipal Incorporation," 80.

34 Tocqueville, *Democracy in America*, 57.

35 *Willard v. Newburyport*, 12 Pick. (Mass) 231 (1831).

36 Morison, *Builders of the Bay Colony*, 90.

37 Ibid., 95.

38 Bremer, *John Winthrop: Biography as History*, 55, 86.

39 Sly, *Town Government in Massachusetts*, 5ff.

40 Morgan, *Founding of Massachusetts*, 76, 82, 92, 96, 109, 114, 190.

41 Parrington, *Colonial Mind*, 42.

42 Ibid., 47.

43 J. Dorfman, *The Economic Mind in American Civilization, 1606–1865* (New York: Viking, 1946), 63.

44 Haskins, *Law and Authority*, 39.

45 M. Zuckerman, *Peaceable Kingdoms* (New York: Knopf, 1970), 139, see G. Liebmann, *Neighborhood Futures: Citizen Rights and Local Control* (New Brunswick, NJ: Transaction Books, 1970), 100–4.

46 Bremer, *John Winthrop: Biography as History*, 38.

47 Quoted in ibid., 85–6; *Winthrop Papers*, III, 463.

48 See the General Court's Order of May 1637, *Winthrop Papers*, III, 422.

49 J. Martin, *Profits in the Wilderness: Entrepreneurship and the Founding of New England Towns in the Seventeenth Century* (Chapel Hill, NC: University of North California Press, 1991).

50 Dorfman, *Economic Mind in American Civilization*, 65.

51 R. Middleton and A. Lombard, *Colonial America: A History to 1763* (Oxford: Wiley-Blackwell, 4th edn., 2011), 186.

52 B. Janniskee, *Local Government in Early America* (Lanham, MD: Rowman & Littlefield, 2011), 130.

53 Rutman, *Winthrop's Boston*, 21.

54 Ibid., 277.

55 R. Hanson, *The Political Thicket: Reapportionment and Constitutional Democracy* (New York: Prentice Hall, 1966), 132.

56 L. Mumford, *The City in History* (Harmondsworth: Penguin, 1961), 331.

57 J. Bryce, *American Commonwealth* (New York: Macmillan, 1895), vol. I, 591.

58 R. Wiebe, *Self Rule: A Cultural History of American Democracy* (Chicago: University of Chicago Press, 1995), 26.

59 Ibid., 31.

3. Thomas Jefferson and the Midwestern Township

1 M. Peterson (ed.), *Jefferson: Writings* (New York: Library of America, 1984), 336ff.

2 W. Ford (ed.), *Journals of the Continental Congress 1774–1789* (Washington, DC: Library of Congress, 1904–37), vol. V, 688 n.1.

3 J. Hurst, *Law and Social Order in the United States* (Ithaca, NY: Cornell University Press, 1977), 114.

4 Peterson, *Jefferson: Writings*, 376ff.

5 *Scott v. Sandford*, 60 U.S. (19 How.) 393, 430–1 (1857).

6 M. Peterson, *Thomas Jefferson and the New Nation* (New York: Oxford University Press, 1970), 283.

7 A. Bestor, "Constitutionalism and the Settlement of the West," in J. Bloom (ed.), *The American Territorial System* (Athens, OH: Ohio State University Press, 1973), 31.

8 J. Boyd (ed.), *The Papers of Thomas Jefferson* (Princeton, NJ: Princeton University Press, 1952), vol. VI, 613, 615.

9 Ibid., VII, 140.

10 T. Jefferson, *Jefferson: Political Writings* (J. Appleby and T. Ball, eds) (Cambridge: Cambridge University Press, 1997), 107.

11 J. Boyd (ed.), *The Papers of Thomas Jefferson* (Princeton, NJ: Princeton University Press, 1952), vol. VI, 616.

12 P. Ford (ed.), *Writings of Thomas Jefferson* (New York: G.P. Putnam's Sons, 1892–9), vol. II, 220–37; A. Koch and W. Piden, *The Life and Selected*

Writings of Thomas Jefferson (New York: Modern Library, 1944), 661–2; R. Honeywell, *The Educational Work of Thomas Jefferson* (Cambridge, MA: Harvard University Press, 1931), ch. 2, app.

13 Jefferson to Monroe, July 9, 1786, in Boyd (ed.), *Papers of Thomas Jefferson*, vol. X, 113.

14 Boyd, *Papers of Thomas Jefferson*, VI, 593.

15 Jefferson to Monroe, July 9, 1786; Jefferson to Madison, December 16, 1786, in ibid., 603.

16 P. Onuf, *Statehood and Union: A History of the Northwest Ordinance* (Bloomington, IN: Indiana University Press, 1987), 38–9.

17 Jefferson to Monroe, June 20, 1787, in Boyd (ed.), *Papers of Thomas Jefferson*, vol. XI, 480.

18 Report of Secretary of State on Executive Proceedings in Northwest Territory, December 14, 1790, in ibid., vol. XVIII, 188.

19 Washington to St. Clair, January 2, 1791, in ibid., 171.

20 Peterson, *Jefferson and the New Nation*, 781.

21 Jefferson to William Short, April 13, 1820, in A. Lipscomb and A. Bergh (eds), *The Writings of Thomas Jefferson* (Washington, DC: Thomas Jefferson Memorial Assn., 1903), vol. XV, 243.

22 Jefferson to Lafayette, December 16, 1820, in ibid., 243.

23 I. Berlin, *Slaves Without Masters: The Free Negro in the Ante-bellum South* (New York: Pantheon, 1975).

24 R. Johannsen, "Stephen A. Douglas and the Territories in the Senate," in Bloom (ed.), *American Territorial System*, 77ff.

25 P. Onuf, *Jefferson's Empire* (Charlottesville, VA: University Press of Virginia, 2000).

26 J. Richardson, *Messages and Papers of the Presidents* (Washington, DC: GPO, 1907), vol. II, 306.

27 P. Gates, *History of Public Land Law Development* (Washington, DC: GPO, 1968). See generally C. Carter (ed.), *Territorial Papers of the United States* (Washington, DC: GPO, 1934–52), 24 vols.

28 Gates, *History of Public Land Law Development*.

29 Peterson, *Jefferson: Writings*, 518.

30 R. Burkhofer, "Jefferson, the Ordinance of 1784 and the Origins of the American Territorial System," 29 *William and Mary Quarterly* (3rd Series) 231 (1972).

31 Gates, *History of Public Land Law Development*, 243.

32 A. De Tocqueville, *Democracy in America* (P. Bradley ed.) (New York: Knopf, 1946), vol. I, 431.

33 Gates, *History of Public Land Law Development*.

34 Hurst, *Law and Social Order*, 13.

35 M. Lanza, *Agrarianism and Reconstruction Politics: The Southern Homestead Act* (Baton Rouge, LA: Louisiana State University Press, 1990), 89, 124.

36 Annual Report of the Commissioner of the Public Land Office for the Fiscal Year Ending June 30, 1890, 3.

37 H. Hedges, "Economic Aspects of the Cattle Industry of the Nebraska Sandhills," quoted in Gates, *History of Public Land Law Development*, 501.

38 B. Cannon, *Reopening the Frontier: Homesteading in the Modern West* (Topeka, KS: University Press of Kansas, 2009).

39 Gates, *History of Public Land Law Development*, 211.

40 M. Primack, "Land Clearing Under Nineteenth Century Techniques," 22 *Journal of Economic History* 484–97 (1962).

41 Minnesota Commissioner of Statistics, *Minnesota: Its Place Among the States* (Hartford, MN: State of Minnesota, 1860), 88, quoted in J. Atack, F. Bateman, and W. Parker, "Northern Agriculture and the Westward Movement," in S. Engerman and R. Gallman (eds), *The Cambridge Economic History of the United States, Vol. II: The Long Nineteenth Century* (Cambridge: Cambridge University Press, 2000), 285, 313.

42 J. Atack *et al.*, "Northern Agriculture and the Westward Movement," 301 and authorities there cited.

43 Ibid., 327–8.

4. Albert Gallatin and Municipal Enterprise

1 L. White, *The Jeffersonians: A Study in Administrative History* (New York: Macmillan, 1951), 493.

2 *American State Papers* (Washington, DC: Gales and Seaton, 1832), vol. I, Miscellaneous, 725.

3 E. Monkkonen, *America Becomes Urban* (Berkeley: University of California Press, 1985).

4 N. Burns, *The Formation of American Local Governments* (New York: Oxford University Press, 1994), 53; see F. Roosevelt, *Public Papers and Addresses of Franklin D. Roosevelt* (New York: Random House, 1938), vol. I, 123.

5 T. Reed, *Municipal Government in the United States* (revised edn.) (New York: Appleton, 1934), 60.

6 N. Lamoreaux, "Entrepreneurship, Organization, and Economic Concentration," in S. Engerman and R. Gallman (eds), *The Cambridge Economic History of the United States, Vol. II: The Long Nineteenth Century* (Cambridge: Cambridge University Press, 2000), 410, 414.

7 H. Adams, *History of the United States During the Administrations of James Madison* (New York: Library of America reprint, 1987), vol. II, 1296–7.

8 J. Madison, Veto Message, March 3, 1817, in J. Richardson (ed.), *Messages and Papers of the Presidents, 1789–1897* (Washington, DC: GPO, 1896), vol. I, 584.

9 J. Monroe, First Annual Message, December 2, 1817, in Richardson (ed.), *Messages and Papers of the Presidents*, II, 11, 18.

10 *Report of the Secretary of the Treasury on the Subject of Public Roads and Canals, April 4, 1808* (Washington, DC: William A. Davis, 1816).

11 *Report of the Secretary of the Treasury on the Subject of Public Roads and Canals, 1808* (repr.) (New York: Augustus M. Kelley, 1968), 73.

12 R. Wiebe, *Self Rule: A Cultural History of American Democracy* (Chicago: University of Chicago Press, 1995), 22.

13 H. Adams, *Life of Albert Gallatin* (New York: Lippincott, 1879), 352.

14 Ibid., 350.

15 A. Balinky, *Albert Gallatin: Fiscal Theories and Policies* (New Brunswick, NJ: Rutgers University Press, 1958), 238.

16 Adams, *History of the United States*, 604, 615.

17 Ibid., 1127, 1177.

18 J. Davis, *Essays in the Earlier History of American Corporations* (Cambridge, MA: Harvard University Press, 1917), vol. I, 53.

19 Ibid., 60.

20 Ibid., 84.

21 Ibid., 87.

22 Ibid., 106.

23 Davis, *Essays in the Earlier History of American Corporations*, II, 17.

24 Ibid., 118.

25 Ibid., 123.

26 Ibid., 135.

27 Ibid., 185.

28 Ibid., 188.

29 Ibid., 216.

30 Fulton to Gallatin, December 8, 1807, in ibid., 123.

31 H. Adams, *Life of Albert Gallatin* (repr.) (New York: Peter Smith, 1943), 355.

32 R. Lively, "The American System: A Review Article," 29 *Business History Review* 81 (1966).

33 R. Briffault, "Our Localism," 90 *Columbia Law Review* 1, 74 n.314 (1990), citing the 1982 U.S. Census of Governments.

34 M. Heath, "Public Railroad Construction and the Development of Private Enterprise in the South before 1861," 10 *Journal of Economic History*, Supplement, 40 (1950).

35 C. Goodrich, *Government Promotion of American Canals and Railroads, 1800–1890* (New York: Columbia University Press, 1960), 42–5.

36 Ibid., 57.

37 Ibid., 272ff.

38 Ibid., 199–200.

39 Ibid., 97.

40 Lively, "The American System," 89, 93.

41 R. Sylla, "Experimental Federalism: The Economics of American Government, 1789–1914," in Engerman and Gallman (eds), *The Cambridge Economic History of the United States*, II, 526.

42 D. Axelrod, *Shadow Government: The Hidden World of Public Authorities* (New York: Wiley, 1992).

43 Ibid., 492.

44 Monkkonen, *America Becomes Urban*.

45 Editorial, *Wall Street Journal*, December 10, 1986, quoted in D. Harloe, *New Ideas for Housing: The Experience of Three Countries* (London: Shelter, 1990), 92.

46 C. Lindblom, "Concepts of Community with Implications for Community Action," unpublished paper (1968), 17.

47 *President's Research Committee on Social Trends, Recent Social Trends* (New York: McGraw-Hill, 1933).

48 E.g. National Resources Planning Board, *Public Works and Rural Land Use* (Washington, DC: GPO, 1942).

5. William Leggett and the General Incorporation Laws

1 A. Du Bois, *English Business Corporations after the Bubble Act* (New York: Columbia University Press, 1938).

2 J. Simeone, "Reassessing Jacksonian Political Culture: William Leggett's Egalitarianism," 4 *American Political Thought* No. 3 (2015).

3 "William Leggett," in *Appleton's Cyclopedia of American Biography* (New York: Appleton & Co., 1888), vol. III, 679.

4 J. Wilson, *Bryant and His Friends* (New York: Fords, Howard and Hulbert, 1886).

5 R. Hofstadter, "William Leggett: Spokesman of Jacksonian Democracy," 58 *Political Science Quarterly* 581 (1943). See also L. White, "William Leggett: Jacksonian Editorialist as Classical Liberal Political Economist," 18 *History of Political Economy* 307 (1986); P. Procter, "William Leggett: Journalist and Literator," 44 *Papers of the Bibliographical Society of America* 239 (1950); C. Degler, "The Loco-Focos: Urban Agendas," 16 *Journal of Economic History* 322 (1957).

6 W. Trimble, "Diverging Tendencies in New York Democracy: The Period of the Loco-Focos," 24 *American Historical Review* 396 (1919).

7 J. Sklansky, *The Melodrama of Panic: William Leggett and the Literary Logic of Jacksonian Political Economy* (2007), at www.ibrarian.net/navon/paper/The_Melodrama_of_Panic__William_Leggett_and_the_L.pdf?paperid=8126027.

8 T. Sedgwick, Jr. (ed.), *A Collection of the Political Writings of William Leggett* (New York: Taylor and Dodd, 1840) [hereafter *Political Writings*], vol. I, 83–4, 106, 143; *Plaindealer*, January 14, 1837, I, 100–1; February

18, 1837, I, 178–9; March 4, 1837, I, 210–13. For the prehistory of Jacksonian debates over chartered corporations, see P. Maier, "The Revolutionary Origins of the American Corporation," 50 *William and Mary Quarterly* (3rd Series) 51 (1993).

9   W. Leggett, "Joint Stock Partnership Law," *New York Evening Post*, December 30, 1834, in L. White (ed.), *W. Leggett, Democratic Editorials: Essays in Jacksonian Political Economy* (Indianapolis: Liberty Press, 1984).

10   *Political Writings*, I, 91–2, 103, 257.

11   *Political Writings*, I, 78, 233; M. Meyers, "A Free Trade Version: William Leggett," in *The Jacksonian Persuasion: Politics and Belief* (Stanford, CA: Stanford University Press, 1957), 141–56.

12   M. Zakim and G. Kornblith (eds), *Capitalism Takes Command: The Social Transformation of Nineteenth-Century America* (Chicago: University of Chicago Press, 2012), 211, quoting *Political Writings*, I, 21.

13   W. Leggett, "Monopolies," *New York Evening Post*, November 20, 1834, in White (ed.), *W. Leggett, Democratic Editorials*, 282.

14   W. Leggett, "Monopolies II," *New York Evening Post*, November 29, 1834, in ibid., 295.

15   W. Leggett, "Free Trade Post Office," *New York Evening Post*, March 23, 1835, in ibid., 306.

16   W. Leggett, "Free Trade Post Office," *Plaindealer*, February 4, 1837, in ibid., 362.

17   "Revolutionary Pensioners," *New York Evening Post*, December 8, 1834.

18   "Literary Corps," *New York Evening Post*, November 26, 1834.

19   W. Trimble, "The Social Philosophy of the Loco-Foco Democracy," 26 *American Journal of Sociology* 705, 711 (1921); Trimble, "Diverging Tendencies."

20   J. Whittier, *Old Portraits and Modern Sketches* (Boston: Ticknor and Fields, 1850), 197.

21   "Leggett's Monument," in J. Whittier, *The Writings of John Greenleaf Whittier in Seven Volumes* (Cambridge, MA: Riverside, 1888), vol. IV, 22.

22   W. Bryant, "In Memory of William Leggett," in L. Untermeyer (ed.), *The Poetry of William Cullen Bryant* (New York: Limited Editions Club, 1947), 142.

23   A. Schlesinger, *The Age of Jackson* (Boston: Little, Brown, 1945), 426. See also S. Wilentz, "Jacksonian Abolitionist," in J. Diggins, *The Liberal Persuasion* (Princeton, NJ: Princeton University Press, 1997); L. Gunn, *The Decline of Authority* (Ithaca, NY: Cornell University Press, 1988); M. Merrill, "The Anticapitalist Origins of the United States," 13 *Review* 465 (1990); Trimble, "The Social Philosophy of the Loco-Foco Democracy"; F. Turner, *The United States, 1830–1850* (New York: Holt, 1935); R. McGrane, *The Panic of 1837* (Chicago: University of Chicago Press, 1924), ch. 5.

24 L. White, "Preface," in White (ed.), *W. Leggett, Democratic Editorials*, xvii.

25 T. Sedgwick, "Preface," in *Political Writings*, I, xvii.

26 Ibid., ix.

27 Ibid., II, 335.

28 *Political Writings*, II, 221–4.

29 F. Byrdsall, *The History of the Loco-Foco or Equal Rights Party* (New York: Burt Franklin, 1967 reprint of 1842 edition).

30 See B. Hammond, "Free Banks and Corporations: The New York Free Banking Act of 1838," 44 *Journal of Political Economy* 184 (1936).

31 White, "Preface."

32 E. Spann, *Ideals and Politics: New York Intellectuals and Liberal Democracy, 1820–1880* (Albany, NY: State University of New York Press, 1972), 100ff.

33 Ibid., 67.

34 W. Leggett, "Stock Gambling," *New York Evening Post*, March 25, 1835, in White (ed.), *W. Leggett, Democratic Editorials*.

35 W. Leggett, "Small Note Circulation," *New York Evening Post*, August 6, 1834, in ibid., 73.

36 W. Leggett, "The Crisis," *Plaindealer*, May 13, 1837, in ibid., 130.

37 W. Leggett, "Foreign Paupers," *Plaindealer*, July 22, 1837, in ibid., 270.

38 W. Leggett, "Sale of Publick Lands," *Plaindealer*, January 14, 1837, in ibid., 351.

39 A. Bickel (ed.), *The Unpublished Opinions of Mr. Justice Brandeis* (Chicago: University of Chicago Press, 1967), 119, 141–4.

40 W. Leggett, "A Little Free Trade Crazy," *New York Evening Post*, December 13, 1834, in White (ed.), *W. Leggett, Democratic Editorials*, 285.

41 W. Leggett, "Meek and Gentle with these Butchers," *Plaindealer*, February 18, 1837, in ibid., 372.

42 Spann, *Ideals and Politics*, 108.

43 Ibid., 109.

44 T. Cochran and W. Miller, *The Age of Enterprise* (New York: Macmillan, 1943), 70.

45 E. Dodd, *American Business Corporations before 1860* (Cambridge, MA: Belknap Press, 1954).

46 J. Hurst, *Legitimacy of the Business Corporation in the Law of the United States, 1780–1970* (Charlottesville, VA: University Press of Virginia, 2014), 69–75.

47 Ibid., 75.

48 R. Nelson, "Privatizing the Neighborhood," in D. Beito, P. Gordon, A. Tabarrok, and Centre for Civil Society (eds), *The Voluntary City: Markets, Communities, and Urban Planning* (New Delhi: Academic Foundation, 2002), 357.

49 Hurst, *Legitimacy of the Business Corporation*, 158–60.
50 E.g. *Liggett v. Baldridge*, 278 U.S. 105 (1928).
51 *Liggett Co. v. Lee*, 288 U.S.517, 541 (1933) (Brandeis, J., dissenting).
52 Hurst, *Legitimacy of the Business Corporation*, 162.
53 *Dodge v. Ford*, 204 Mich. 459, 170 N.W.668 (1919); see *eBay Domestic Holdings, Inc. v. Neumark*, 16 A.3rd 1 Del.Ch. (2010); see "Benefit Corporations: Pursuit of Purpose Alongside Profit," *Financial Times*, October 15, 2012.
54 R. Arne, "Entrepreneurial City Planning," in D. Beito *et al.* (eds), *The Voluntary City*, 156.

6. Justin Morrill and Land Grant Colleges

1   E. Eddy, *Colleges for Our Land and Time: The Land Grant Idea in American Education* (New York: Harper, 1957). See C. Cross, *Justin Smith Morrill: Father of the Land Grant Colleges* (East Lansing, MI: Michigan State University Press, 1999); W. Parker, *The Life and Public Services of Justin Smith Morrill* (Boston: Houghton Mifflin, 1927).
2   Quoted in D. Boorstin, *The Americans: The Democratic Experience* (New York: Vintage, 1974), 487.
3   Cross, *Justin Smith Morrill*, 35–7.
4   Ibid., n.49.
5   Ibid., 79–81.
6   Ibid., 118–19.
7   Ibid., 64.
8   Ibid., 121.
9   A. Nevins, *The State Universities and Democracy* (Urbana, IL: University of Illinois Press, 1962).
10 Chapter 130 of the Acts of 1862, 12 Stat. 593 (1862).
11 E. Ross, *Democracy's College: The Land Grant Movement in the Formative Stage* (New York: Arno, 1969).
12 Cross, *Justin Smith Morrill*.
13 Boorstin, *The Americans*, 484–7.
14 R. Williams, *The Origins of Federal Support for Higher Education: George W. Atherton and the Land Grant College Movement* (University Park, PA: Penn State University Press, 1991); G. Anderson (ed.), *Land-Grant Universities: Their Continuing Challenge* (Lansing, MI: Michigan State University Press, 1976).
15 Committee on the Centennial of the University of Illinois, *An Early View of the Land Grant Colleges* (Urbana, IL: University of Illinois, 1967), 50.
16 R. Scott, *The Reluctant Farmer: The Rise of Agricultural Extension to 1949* (Urbana, IL: University of Illinois Press, 1971); W. Rasmussen,

Taking the University to the People (Ames, IA: Iowa State University Press, 1989).

17 S. Morison and H. Commager, *The Growth of the American Republic* (New York: Oxford University Press, 4th edn., 1955), 196.

18 [British] Academies Act 2010, ch. 32.

19 D. Ross, *Preparing for Ulysses* (New York: Columbia University Press, 1969), 271.

20 M. Bennett, *When Dreams Came True: The GI Bill and the Making of Modern America* (Washington, DC: Brassey's, 1996), 243–5.

21 Ross, *Preparing for Ulysses*, 123.

22 S. Levitan, *Swords into Plowshares: Our G.I. Bill* (Salt Lake City, UT: Olympus Pub. Co., 1973), ch. 8.

23 38 U.S.C.A. sec. 3001ff.

24 T. Skocpol, "The G.I. Bill and U.S. Social Policy, Past and Future", 14(2) *Social Policy and Philosophy* 95–115 (1997).

7. John Wesley Powell and Western Public Lands

1 G. Merrill, "John Wesley Powell," in *Dictionary of American Biography* (New York: Scribner, 1925), vol. VIII, 146.

2 J. Terrell, *The Man Who Rediscovered America: A Biography of John Wesley Powell* (New York: Weybright and Talley, 1969), 219, 231.

3 J. Powell, *Report on the Lands of the Arid Region of the United States* (Cambridge, MA: Harvard University Press, 1962).

4 Ibid., 42.

5 Ibid., 40.

6 Ibid., 45.

7 Ibid., 47, 50.

8 L. Mumford, *The City in History* (Harmondsworth: Penguin, 1961), 331.

9 Powell, *Report*, 34–5, 36.

10 Ibid. (Preface by Wallace Stegner, citing J. Hedges, *Building the Canadian West: The Land and Colonization Policies of the Canadian Pacific Railway* (New York: Macmillan, 1939)).

11 Ibid., 41.

12 Ibid., 50.

13 Ibid., 51–5, 52.

14 Ibid., 33 (Preface by Wallace Stegner).

15 Ibid., 54, 55.

16 D. Fowler, "John Wesley Powell," in *American National Biography* (New York: Oxford University Press, 1999), vol. XVII, 780. See also D. Worster, *A River Running West: The Life of John Wesley Powell* (New York: Oxford University Press, 2002); J. Aton, *John Wesley Powell: His Life and Legacy* (Salt Lake City, UT: University of Utah Press, 2009).

17 Terrell, *The Man Who Rediscovered America*, 7–8.
18 P. Gates, *History of Public Land Law Development* (Washington, DC: GPO, 1978), 652.
19 Ibid., 656.
20 Ibid., 654.
21 P. Gates, "California's Embattled Settlers," in *The Jeffersonian Dream: Studies in the History of American Land Policy and Development* (Albuquerque, NM: University of New Mexico Press, 1996), 56, 78; see also P. Gates, "Adjudication of Spanish-Mexican Land Claims in California," 21 *Huntington Library Quarterly* 213ff. (May 1958).
22 Gates, *History of Public Land Law Development*, 653.
23 P. Gates, "Corporation Farming in California," in P. Gates, *Land and Law in California* (Ames, IA: Iowa State University Press, 1993), 329, 348. See M. Reisner, *Cadillac West: The American West and Its Disappearing Water* (New York: Penguin, 1993).
24 J. Gunther, *Inside USA* (London: Hamish Hamilton, 1947), 38.
25 Gates, *The Jeffersonian Dream*, 121, 139.
26 B. Hibbard, *A History of the Public Land Policies* (New York: Macmillan, 1924), 567, 569–70.
27 Ibid., 528–9.
28 E. Peffer, *The Closing of the Public Domain: Disposal and Reservation Policies, 1900–1950* (Stanford, CA: Stanford University Press, 1951), 339.
29 See J. Gance, "The Desert Land Act in Operation," 11 *Agricultural History* 142 (1937); J. Gance, "The Desert Land Act Since 1891," 11 *Agricultural History* 266 (1937).
30 K. Stringfellow, *Jackrabbit Homestead: Tracing the Small Tract Act in the Southern California Landscape, 1938–2008* (Chicago: University of Chicago Press, 2009), citing "Filed by Movie Stars, Notables," *Desert Trail Magazine*, February 16, 1945, 16 n.16.
31 Ibid., 293.
32 Gates, *The Jeffersonian Dream*, 125.
33 J. Bryce, *The American Commonwealth* (New York: Macmillan, 1895), vol. II, 838–9.
34 Terrell, *The Man Who Rediscovered America*, 138.
35 Ibid., 226.
36 Ibid., 172.
37 Ibid., 228.

8. Joseph Pulitzer and Municipal Home Rule

1 D. Seitz, *Joseph Pulitzer: His Life and Letters* (London: Geoffrey Bles, 1926), 64–72.
2 J. Morris, *Pulitzer: A Life in Politics, Print and Power* (New York: Harper, 2010), 116.

3 T. Barclay, *The Movement for Municipal Home Rule in St. Louis*, 18 University of Missouri Studies No. 2 (Columbia, MO: University of Missouri, 1943), 62–3.

4 Morris, *Pulitzer*, 116.

5 Barclay, *The Movement for Municipal Home Rule in St. Louis*, 75–6.

6 Ibid., 36, 38.

7 J. Teaford, *The Unheralded Triumph: City Government in America, 1870–1900* (Baltimore, MD: Johns Hopkins University Press, 1984), 106.

8 Seitz, *Joseph Pulitzer*, 85.

9 Barclay, *The Movement for Municipal Home Rule in St. Louis*, 77, quoting H. McBain, *The Law and the Practice of Municipal Home Rule* (New York: Columbia University Press, 1916), 113.

10 Barclay, *The Movement for Municipal Home Rule in St. Louis*, 80.

11 Ibid., 84.

12 Ibid., 78.

13 I. Loeb and F. Shoemaker (eds), *Debates of the Missouri Constitutional Convention of 1875* (Columbia, MO: State Historical Society of Missouri, 1944), vol. I, 501.

14 Ibid.

15 Loeb and Shoemaker, *Debates*, vol. XII, 449, 462, 468, 470–1.

16 C. Patton, *The Battle for Municipal Reform: Mobilization and Attack, 1875 to 1900* (College Park, MD: McGrath Pub. Co., 1969), 65–6.

17 Barclay, *The Movement for Municipal Home Rule in St. Louis*, 86, n.59.

18 Ibid., 109.

19 Ibid., 109ff.

20 *Debates and Proceedings of the Constitutional Convention of the State of California* (Sacramento, CA: State Printing Office, 1881), vol. III, 1407.

21 H. Deming, *The Government of American Cities: A Program of Democracy* (New York: Putnam, 1909), 94–5.

22 W. Anderson, *American City Government* (London: Pitman, 1924), 60.

23 See F. Stewart, *A Half Century of Municipal Reform: The History of the National Municipal League* (Berkeley, CA: University of California Press, 1950).

24 These are set out in Deming, *The Government of American Cities*, 239–304.

25 Loeb and Shoemaker, *Debates*, XII, 52.

26 Patton, *The Battle for Municipal Reform*, 16–17.

27 Teaford, *The Unheralded Triumph*, 121–2.

28 Ibid., 312–13.

29 *St. Louis v. Western Union Tel. Co.*, 149 U.S. 465 (1893) (Brewer, J.).

30 K. Valandingham, "Constitutional Municipal Home Rule," 17 *William and Mary Law Review* 1 (1975).

31 J. Frug, "The City as a Legal Concept," 93 *Harvard Law Review*
    1057 (1980); T. Sandalow, "The Limits of Municipal Power under
    Home Rule: A Role for the Courts," 48 *Minnesota Law Review* 643
    (1964).
32 R. Briffault, "Our Localism," 90 *Columbia Law Review* 1, 346 (1990).
33 T. Barclay, "What Municipal Home Rule Means Today: Missouri," 21
    National Municipal Review 312 (1932).
34 Morris, *Pulitzer*, 118. See W. Cassella, "City-County Separation: The
    'Great Divorce' of 1876," 15 *Missouri Historical Society Bulletin* No. 2
    (1959).
35 *Kansas City ex rel Northern Park District v. Scarritt*, 127 Mo. 642
    (1894).
36 Quoted in Seitz, *Joseph Pulitzer*, 85–6.
37 M. Gunther, *The Wealthy 100: From Benjamin Franklin to Bill Gates—A
    Ranking of the Richest Americans, Past and Present* (Secaucus, NJ: Carol
    Pub. Group, 1996).
38 Quoted in E. Kirschten, *Catfish and Crystal* (Garden City, NY:
    Doubleday, 1960), 264.
39 E. Griffith: *A History of American City Government, Vol. IV: The
    Progressive Years and Their Aftermath, 1900–1920* (New York: Praeger,
    1974), 256, 313.
40 R. Briffault, "A Government for Our Time: Business Improvement
    Districts and Urban Governance," 99 *Columbia Law Review* 365
    (1999).
41 J. Garreau, *Edge City: Life on the New Frontier* (New York: Anchor, 1992).
42 G. Liebmann, "The New American Local Government," 34 *Urban Lawyer*
    93 (2002).
43 [British] Local Government and Rating Act 1997, ch. 29; Localism Act
    2011, ch. 20.

9. Hugh Hammond Bennett and Soil Conservation Districts

1 R. Morgan, *Governing Soil Conservation: Thirty Years of the New
   Decentralization* (Baltimore, MD: Johns Hopkins University Press,
   1965), 285ff.
2 W. Brink, *Big Hugh: The Father of Soil Conservation* (New York:
   Macmillan, 1951).
3 J. Daniels, *Tar Heels: The Story of North Carolina* (New York: Dodd
   Mead, 1941).
4 Obituary, *New York Times*, July 8, 1960; M. Cook, *Hugh Hammond
   Bennett: The Father of Soil Conservation*, at www.soil.ncsu.edu/about/
   century/hugh.html; D. Helms, "Hugh Hammond Bennett and the
   Creation of the Soil Conservation Service, September 19, 1933–April

27, 1935," Natural Resources Conservation Service, Historical Insights No. 9 (March 2010) [hereafter Helms, I]; see also D. Helms, "Hugh Hammond Bennett and the Creation of the Soil Erosion Service," Natural Resources Conservation Service, Historical Insights No. 8 (September 2008); D. Helms, "Hugh Hammond Bennett and the Creation of the Soil Erosion Service," 6 *Journal of Soil and Water Conservation* No. 2 (March–April 2009), 68A–74A; C. Agles, "Hugh Bennett," in W. Powell (ed.), *Dictionary of North Carolina Biography* (Chapel Hill, NC: University of North Carolina Press, 1988), vol. I; L. Fuller, "Hugh H. Bennett," *Dictionary of American Biography*, Supplement Six, 1956–60 (New York: Scribner, 1980), 53; D. Helms, "Hugh H. Bennett," in *American National Biography* (New York: Oxford University Press, 1999), vol. II, 582.

5 D. Simms, *The Soil Conservation Service* (New York: Praeger, 1971), 5.

6 C. Hardin, *The Politics of Agriculture: Soil Conservation and the Struggle for Power in Rural America* (Glencoe, IL: Free Press, 1952), 97ff.

7 D. Simms, *The Soil Conservation Service*, 5.

8 Brink, *Big Hugh*, 17.

9 Ibid., 14.

10 Ibid.

11 Ibid.

12 B. Dodson, "A Soil Conservation Safari: Hugh Bennett's 1944 Visit to South Africa," 11 *Environment and History* 35 (2006).

13 Brink, *Big Hugh*, 88.

14 Hardin, *The Politics of Agriculture*, 71.

15 B. Rauch, *The History of the New Deal, 1933–38* (New York: Capricorn Books, 1963), 214–15.

16 Brink, *Big Hugh*, 9.

17 Hardin, *The Politics of Agriculture*, 86.

18 A. Griswold, *Farming and Democracy* (New Haven, CT: Yale University Press, 1952), 185.

19 R. Hurt, *The Big Empty: The Great Plains in the Twentieth Century* (Tucson, AZ: University of Arizona Press, 2011), 104–12.

20 D. Gangbill, "Twenty Years of Global Re Leaf," 114 *American Forester*, Issue 3, 7 (2008).

21 Brink, *Big Hugh*, 117.

22 Morgan, *Governing Soil Conservation*, 285ff.

23 Hardin, *The Politics of Agriculture*, 103.

24 Brink, *Big Hugh*, 128ff.

25 M. Stewart, "Cultivating Kudzu: The Soil Conservation Service and the Kudzu Distribution Program," 81 *Georgia Historical Quarterly* 151 (1997). See H. Bennett, *Elements of Soil Conservation* (New York: McGraw-Hill, 2nd edn., 1955), 181, 219.

26 H. Bennett and W. Pryor, *This Land We Defend* (New York: Longman's, 1942).
27 See E. Ferguson, "Nationwide Erosion Control, Soil Conservation Districts, and the Power of Land Use Regulation," 34 *Iowa Law Review* 166 (1949).
28 Morgan, *Governing Soil Conservation*, 363.
29 H. Bennett, "Law in Peril: Soil Program Slipping," *The Nation*, May 23, 1953, 436.
30 B. De Voto, "Conservation: Down and On the Way Out," 209 *Harper's* (August 1954), 66.
31 Cook, *Hugh Hammond Bennett*, 10.
32 Helms, I.
33 L. Bromfield, "Preface," to Brink, *Big Hugh*, viii.
34 Bennett, *Elements of Soil Conservation*, 311ff.
35 Hardin, *The Politics of Agriculture*, 268.
36 Brink, *Big Hugh*, 109.
37 General Accounting Office Report RCED-04-241 (September 1994).
38 J. Hagstrom, "Born of the Dust Bowl," *Government Executive*, June 1, 1996.
39 Common Ground, "The SCS once the farmer's helper has become a mighty enforcer," 27 *Government Executive*, June 1, 1996.
40 P. Johnson, "NRCS: Changing to Meet the Future," 94 *Journal of Forestry* 12 (1996).
41 J. Esseks, S. Kraft, and D. Ihrke, "Policy Lessons for a Quasi-Regulatory Conservation Program," in T. Napier, S. Napier, and J. Tvrdon (eds), *Soil and Water Conservation Policies and Programs: Successes and Failures* (Boca Raton, FL: CRC Press, 2000), 110–11.
42 Ibid.
43 D. Hoag, J. Hughes-Popp and P. Huszar, "Is U.S. Soil Conservation Policy a Sustainable Development?," in Napier *et al.* (eds), *Soil and Water Conservation Policies and Programs*, 127–42.
44 D. Cressman, S. Duff, P. Brubacher, and J. Arnold, "Soil Conservation Policy in Canada: Adrift or in a State of Evolution?," and D. Stonehouse, "A Critical Assessment of the Ontario Land Stewardship Program," in Napier *et al.* (eds), *Soil and Water Conservation Policies and Programs*, 169, 191.
45 Brink, *Big Hugh*, 143.
46 I. Hannan, "Soil Conservation Policies in Australia: Successes, Failure, and Requirements for Ecologically Sustainable Policy," and J. Cary, "Successful Soil and Landscape Conservation in Australia," in Napier *et al.* (eds), *Soil and Water Conservation Policies and Programs*, 493, 535.
47 Johnson, "NRCS."
48 D. Conrad, "Implementation of Conservation Title Provisions at the State Level," in Napier *et al.* (eds), *Soil and Water Conservation Policies and Programs*, 66–75.

49 T. Weber and G. Margheim, "Conservation Policy in the U.S.," in Napier *et al.* (eds), *Soil and Water Conservation Policies and Programs*, 51–6.

50 J. Hagstrom, "Common Ground," *Government Executive*, June 1, 1996.

51 H. Bennett, *The Development of Natural Resources: The Coming Technological Revolution on the Land*, October 2, 1946, at ww3.nrcs. usda.gov.

52 M. Schnepf, "Role of Private and Professional Organizations in the Development of Soil and Water Conservation Policy," in T. Napier *et al.* (eds), *Soil and Water Conservation Policies and Programs*, 90ff.

53 P. Singer, "Bush and the Bureaucracy: A Crusade for Control," *Government Executive*, March 25, 2005.

54 M. Schnepf, "Role of Private and Professional Organizations in the Development of Soil and Water Conservation Policy," in T. Napier *et al.* (eds), *Soil and Water Conservation Policies and Programs*, 102.

55 J. Hagstrom, "USDA Considers Consolidation," *Government Executive*, June 24, 1997; J. Hagstrom, "Gathering Storm," *Government Executive*, June 1, 1998.

10. Byron Hanke and the Residential Community Association

1 www.caionline.org, November 1, 2016.

2 G. Liebmann, "The New American Local Government," 34 *Urban Lawyer* 93 (2002).

3 Tex. Code Ann. Property, sec. 203.003.

4 Montgomery County (Md.) Code, sec. 8–24; Anne Arundel County (Md.) Code, sec. 3–2–103.

5 G. Liebmann, *Neighborhood Futures: Citizen Rights and Local Control* (New Brunswick, NJ: Transaction Books, 2003), 163–4.

6 D. Stabile, *Community Associations: The Emergence and Acceptance of a Quiet Innovation in Housing* (Westport, CT: Greenwood Press, 2000), 81–3.

7 41 Eng. Rep. 1143 (Ch., 1848).

8 Stabile, *Community Associations*, 49–55.

9 Ibid., 60.

10 Ibid., 82, citing H. Lautner (ed.), *Subdivision Regulations: An Analysis of Land Subdivision Land Control Practices* (Chicago: Public Administration Service, 1941).

11 B. Hanke and A. Faure, *Suggested Land Subdivision Regulations* (Washington, DC: Housing and Home Finance Agency, 1952).

12 Ibid., 53, quoted in Stabile, *Community Associations*, 84.

13 Stabile, *Community Associations*, 84.

14 D. Clurman and E. Hebard, *Condominiums and Cooperatives* (New York: Wiley, 1970).

15 B. Hanke *et al.*, *Planned Unit Development with a Homes Association*, FHA Land Planning Bulletin 6 (Washington, DC: HUD, 1963).

16 Stabile, *Community Associations*, 90.

17 B. Hanke, "Planned Unit Development and Land Use Intensity," 114 *University of Pennsylvania Law Review* 1 (1965) and the literature cited in Stabile, *Community Associations*, 110 n. 26.

18 Stabile, *Community Associations*, 105.

19 C. Rose, "The Comedy of the Commons," 53 *University of Chicago Law Review* 211, 781 (1986).

20 B. Hanke (ed.), *The Homes Association Handbook* (Washington, DC: Urban Land Institute, 1966).

21 Stabile, *Community Associations*, 102.

22 Ibid., 102–3.

23 R. Drachman, "ULI's 40th Anniversary," *Urban Land* (December 1977), quoted in ibid., 104.

24 Quoted in E. McKenzie, *Privatopia* (New Haven, CT: Yale, 1994), 177.

25 E.g. *City of Eastlake v. Forest City*, 426 U.S. 668, 673 (1976). Interestingly, the earliest draft of the Standard Zoning Enabling Act allowed 20 percent of local residents to require a three-quarters vote of the city council.

26 B. Hanke and R. Ekimoto, *Design Review: How Community Associations Maintain Peace and Harmony* (Arlington, VA: Community Associations Institute, repr. 2004).

27 S. Siegel, "The Public Role in Establishing Private Residential Communities," 38 *Urban Lawyer* 859 (2006); Symposium, "Home Owners' Associations as Private Governments," 21 *Public Administration Review* 535–58 (2011).

28 D. Clurman and E. Hebard, *Condominiums and Cooperatives* (New York: Wiley, 1970).

29 A. Pryce and C. Bruere, *Timeshare Coming of Age* (London: Travel and Tourism Intelligence, 1999), 25.

30 Stabile, *Community Associations*.

31 McKenzie, *Privatopia*, 91, 93. See also E. McKenzie, *Beyond Privatopia: Rethinking Residential Private Government* (Washington, DC: Urban Institute, 2011).

32 Quoted in Stabile, *Community Associations*, 104.

33 Advisory Commission in Intergovernmental Relations, *Residential Community Associations* (Washington, DC: ACIR, 1989), 1, 3, 27.

34 Ibid., 4, 11, 12, 21.

35 Md. Code, Art. 23A, secs. 49–51.

36 Ibid., sec. 2–17, 2–18.

37 Ibid., sec. 3–106, 3–109.

38 G. Liebmann, *Solving Problems without Large Government: Devolution, Fairness, and Equality* (Westport, CT: Praeger, 2000), 20–1.

39 McKenzie, *Privatopia*.

40 K. Jackson, *Crabgrass Frontier: The Suburbanization of the United States* (New York: Oxford University Press, 1985), 195.

41 G. Liebmann, "Suburban Zoning: Two Modest Proposals," 25 *Real Property, Probate and Trust Law Journal* 1 (1990).

42 W. Hyatt, "Common Interest Communities: Evolution and Reinvention," 31 *John Marshall Law School Law Review* 303, 379ff. (1998).

Conclusion: The Way Forward

1 "Chief Justice Hughes Addresses the Judicial Conference of the Fourth Circuit," 18 *American Bar Association Journal* 445 (1932).

2 M. Bennett, *When Dreams Came True: The GI Bill and the Making of Modern America* (Washington, DC: Brassey's, 1996), 317.

3 German Basic Law, Art. 106; D. Currie, *The Constitution of the Federal Republic of Germany* (Chicago: University of Chicago Press, 1994), 52–60; W. Oates, *The Political Economy of Fiscal Federalism* (Lexington, MA: Lexington Books, 1977), 75; Y. Meny, "Financial Transfers and Local Government in France," in D. Ashford (ed.), *Financing Urban Government in the Welfare State* (New York: St. Martin's, 1980); K. Messere, *Tax Policy in OECD Countries* (Amsterdam: BFD Publications, 1993), 202.

4 See A. Rivlin, *Reviving the American Dream* (Washington, DC: Brookings, 1992); R. Strauss, "The EC Challenge to State and Local Governments," 16 *Intergovernmental Perspective* 13 (1990); R. Dahl, *After the Revolution* (New Haven, CT: Yale University Press, 1970), 133–4.

5 D. Kenyon, "A New State VAT: Lessons from New Hampshire," 49 *National Tax Journal* 381 (1996).

6 G. Liebmann, *The Gallows in the Grove: Civil Society in American Law* (Westport, CT: Praeger, 1997), 226–9 and works cited at 242.

7 P. Drucker, *Post Capitalist Society* (New York: Harper, 1993), 112; National Health Service Act, 1946, sec.33; R. Levitt and A. Wall, *The Reorganized National Health Service* (London: Croom Helm, 3rd edn., 1984); R. Klein, *Politics of the National Health Service* (London: Longman, 2nd edn., 1989).

8 Liebmann, *Gallows*, 222–4 and works cited at 242; see also G. Liebmann, "Land Readjustment for America: A Proposal for a Statute," 32 *Urban Lawyer* 1 (2000).

9 M. Castells, *The Shek Kip Mei Syndrome: Economic Development and Public Housing in Hong Kong and Singapore* (London: Pion, 1990), 95–7.

10 A. De Tocqueville, *Democracy in America* (P. Bradley ed.) (New York: Knopf, 1946), vol. I, 90.

11 W. Hurst, *Law and the Conditions of Freedom in the Nineteenth Century United States* (Madison, WI: University of Wisconsin Press, 1956), 7.

12 R. Nelson, "Privatizing the Neighborhood," in D. Beito, P. Gordon, A. Tabarrok, and Centre for Civil Society (eds), *The Voluntary City: Markets, Communities, and Urban Planning* (New Delhi: Academic Foundation, 2002), 411.

13 R. Wiebe, *Self Rule: A Cultural History of American Democracy* (Chicago: University of Chicago Press, 1995), 266.

BIBLIOGRAPHY

Adams, H. *Life of Albert Gallatin* (New York: Lippincott, 1879).
___ *History of the United States during the Administrations of Thomas Jefferson* (New York: Library of America, 1986).
___ *History of the United States during the Administrations of James Madison* (New York: Library of America reprint, 1987).
Advisory Commission in Intergovernmental Relations. *Residential Community Associations* (Washington, DC: ACIR, 1989).
Agles, C. "Hugh Bennett," in W. Powell (ed.), *Dictionary of North Carolina Biography* (Chapel Hill, NC: University of North California Press, 1979), vol. I.
American State Papers (Washington, DC: Gales and Seaton, 1832).
Anderson, G. (ed.). *Land-Grant Universities: Their Continuing Challenge* (Lansing, MI: Michigan State University Press, 1976).
Anderson, W. *American City Government* (London: Pitman, 1924).
Andrews, C. *The Colonial Period of American History* (New Haven, CT: Yale University Press, 1937), vol. III.
Armitage, D. "John Locke, Carolina, and the Two Treatises of Government," 32 *Political Theory* 602 (2004).
Arneil, B. *John Locke and America: The Defence of British Colonialism* (Oxford: Clarendon, 1996).
Ashcraft, R. (ed.). *John Locke: Critical Assessments* (London: Routledge, 1991), vol. I.
Ashford, D. *Financing Urban Government in the Welfare State* (New York: St. Martin's, 1980).
Aton, J. *John Wesley Powell: His Life and Legacy* (Salt Lake City, UT: University of Utah Press, 2009).
Axelrod, D. *Shadow Government: The Hidden World of Public Authorities* (New York: Wiley, 1992).
Balinky, A. *Albert Gallatin: Fiscal Theories and Policies* (New Brunswick, NJ: Rutgers University Press, 1958).
Barclay, T. "What Municipal Home Rule Means Today: Missouri," 21 *National Municipal Review* 312 (1932).

___ *The Movement for Municipal Home Rule in St. Louis*, 18 University of Missouri Studies No. 2 (Columbia, MO: University of Missouri, 1943).

Bazelon, E., and E. Posner. "The Government Gorsuch Wants to Undo: His Judicial Philosophy Would Undermine the Modern Administrative State," *New York Times*, April 2, 2017, Sunday Review.

Beito, D., P. Gordon, A. Tabarrok, and Centre for Civil Society (eds). *The Voluntary City: Choice, Community and Civil Society* (Ann Arbor, MI: University of Michigan Press, 2002).

Bennett, H. "Law in Peril: Soil Program Slipping," *The Nation*, May 23, 1953.

___ *Elements of Soil Conservation* (New York: McGraw-Hill, 2nd edn., 1955).

Bennett, H., and W. Pryor. *This Land We Defend* (New York: Longman's, 1942).

Bennett, M. *When Dreams Came True: The G.I. Bill and the Making of Modern America* (Lincoln, NE: Brassey's, 1999).

Berlin, I. *Slaves without Masters: The Free Negro in the Ante-bellum South* (New York: Pantheon, 1975).

Bloom, J. (ed.). *The American Territorial System* (Athens, OH: Ohio State University Press, 1973).

Boorstin, D. *The Americans: The Democratic Experience* (New York: Vintage, 1974).

Boyd, J. (ed.). *The Papers of Thomas Jefferson* (Princeton, NJ: Princeton University Press, 1952).

Bremer, F. *John Winthrop: America's Forgotten Founding Father* (New York: Oxford University Press, 2003).

___ *John Winthrop: Biography as History* (New York: Continuum, 2009).

Bremer, F., and L. Botelho. *The World of John Winthrop* (Charlottesville, VA: University Press of Virginia, 2005).

Briffault, R. "Our Localism," 90 *Columbia Law Review* 1 (1990).

___ "A Government for Our Time: Business Improvement Districts and Urban Governance," 99 *Columbia Law Review* 365 (1999).

Brink, W. *Big Hugh: The Father of Soil Conservation* (New York: Macmillan, 1951).

Brownell, B., and D. Goldfield (eds). *The City in Southern History* (Port Washington, NY: Kennikat Press, 1977).

Burkhofer, R. "Jefferson, the Ordinance of 1784 and the Origins of the American Territorial System," 29 *William and Mary Quarterly* (3rd Series) 231 (1972).

Burns, N. *The Formation of American Local Governments* (New York: Oxford University Press, 1994).

Byrdsall, F. *The History of the Loco-Foco or Equal Rights Party* (New York: Burt Franklin, 1967, reprint of 1842 edition).

Cannon, B. *Re-opening the Frontier: Homesteading in the Modern West* (Topeka, KS: University Press of Kansas, 2009).

Carter, C. (ed.). *Territorial Papers of the United States* (Washington, DC: GPO, 1934–52), 24 vols.

Cassella, W. "City–County Separation: The 'Great Divorce' of 1876," 15 *Missouri Historical Society Bulletin* No. 2 (1959).

Castells, M. *The Shek Kip Mei Syndrome: Economic Development and Public Housing in Hong Kong and Singapore* (London: Pion, 1990).

Clurman, D., and E. Hebard. *Condominiums and Cooperatives* (New York: Wiley, 1970).

Cochran, T., and W. Miller. *The Age of Enterprise* (New York: Macmillan, 1943).

Committee of the Centennial of the University of Illinois. *An Early View of the Land Grant Colleges* (Urbana, IL: University of Illinois Press, 1967).

Common Ground. "The SCS Once the Farmer's Helper Has Become a Mighty Enforcer," 27 *Government Executive*, June 1, 1996.

Cook, M. *Hugh Hammond Bennett: The Father of Soil Conservation*, at www.soil.ncsu.edu/about/century/hugh.html.

Cranston, M. *John Locke: A Biography* (London: Longmans, 1957).

Craven, W. *The Southern Colonies in the Seventeenth Century, 1607–1689* (Baton Rouge, LA: Louisiana State University Press, 1949).

Cross, C. *Justin Smith Morrill: Father of the Land Grant Colleges* (East Lansing, MI: Michigan State University Press, 1999).

Currie, D. *The Constitution of the Federal Republic of Germany* (Chicago: University of Chicago Press, 1994).

Dahl, R. *After the Revolution* (New Haven, CT: Yale University Press, 1970).

Daniels, J. *Tarheels: The Story of North Carolina* (New York: Dodd Mead, 1941).

Davis, J. *Essays in the Earlier History of American Corporations* (Cambridge, MA: Harvard University Press, 1917), vol. I.

De Beer, E. (ed.). *The Correspondence of John Locke* (Oxford: Clarendon Press, 1976).

De Voto, B. "Conservation: Down and On the Way Out," 209 *Harper's* (August 1954).

Debates and Proceedings of the Constitutional Convention of the State of California (Sacramento: State Printing Office, 1881).

Degler, C. "The Loco-Focos: Urban Agendas," 16 *Journal of Economic History* 322 (1957).

Deming, H. *The Government of American Cities: A Program of Democracy* (New York: Putnam, 1909).

Des Meizeaux, P. (ed.). *A Collection of Several Pieces of Mr. John Locke* (London: R. Francklin, 1st ed., 1720; 2nd ed., 1739).

Diggins, J. *The Liberal Persuasion* (Princeton, NJ: Princeton University Press, 1997).

Dillick, S. *Community Organization for Neighborhood Development* (New York: Morrow, 1953).

Dodd, E. *American Business Corporations before 1860* (Cambridge, MA: Belknap Press, 1954).

Dodson, B. "A Soil Conservation Safari: Hugh Bennett's 1944 Visit to South Africa," 11 *Environment and History* 35 (2006).

Dorfman, J. *The Economic Mind in American Civilization, 1606–1865* (New York: Viking, 1946).

Drachman, R. "ULI's 40th Anniversary," *Urban Land* (December 1977).

Drucker, P. *Post Capitalist Society* (New York: Harper, 1993).

Du Bois, A. *English Business Corporations after the Bubble Act* (New York: Columbia University Press, 1938).

Dunn, R., and L. Yeandle (eds). *The Journal of John Winthrop* (Cambridge, MA: Belknap Press, 1996).

Eaton, A. *Constitution Making in Rhode Island* (Providence, RI: Rhode Island Constitutional League, 1899).

___ "Origins of Municipal Incorporation in England and in the United States," *Proceedings of the American Bar Association*, August 1902.

Eddy, E. *Colleges for Our Land and Time: The Land Grant Idea in American Education* (New York: Harper, 1957).

Edgar, W. *South Carolina: A History* (Columbia, SC: University of South Carolina Press, 1998).

Engerman, S., and R. Gallman (eds). *The Cambridge Economic History of the United States, Vol. I: The Colonial Era* (Cambridge: Cambridge University Press, 1996).

___ *The Cambridge Economic History of the United States, Vol. II: The Long Nineteenth Century* (Cambridge: Cambridge University Press, 2000).

Farr, J. "'So Vile and Miserable an Estate': The Problem of Slavery in Locke's Political Thought," 14 *Political Theory* 263 (1986).

___ "Locke, Natural Law, and New World Slavery," 36 *Political Theory* 495 (2008).

Ferguson, E. "Nationwide Erosion Control, Soil Conservation Districts, and the Power of Land Use Regulation," 34 *Iowa Law Review* 166 (1949).

Ford, W. (ed.). *Journals of the Continental Congress 1774–1789* (Washington, DC: Library of Congress, 1904–37), vol. V.

Fowler, D. "John Wesley Powell," in *American National Biography* (New York: Oxford University Press, 1999), vol. XVII, 780.

Friendly, H. *The Federal Administrative Agencies: The Need for Better Definition of Standards* (Cambridge, MA: Harvard University Press, 1962), reprinted in H. Friendly, *Benchmarks* (Chicago: University of Chicago Press, 1967).

Frug, J. "The City as a Legal Concept," 93 *Harvard Law Review* 1057 (1980).

Fuller, L. "Hugh H. Bennett," in *Dictionary of American Biography*, Supplement Six, 1956–60 (New York: Scribner, 1980).

Gance, J. "The Desert Land Act in Operation," 11 *Agricultural History* 142 (1937).

___ "The Desert Land Act since 1891," 11 *Agricultural History* 266 (1937).

Gangbill, D. "Twenty Years of Global Re Leaf," 114 *American Forester*, Issue 3, 7 (2008).

Garreau, J. *Edge City: Life on the New Frontier* (New York: Anchor, 1992).

Gates, P. "Adjudication of Spanish-Mexican Land Claims in California," 21 *Huntington Library Quarterly* 213 (May 1958).

___ *History of Public Land Law Development* (Washington, DC: GPO, 1978).

___ *Land and Law in California* (Ames, IA: Iowa State University Press, 1993).

___ *The Jeffersonian Dream: Studies in the History of American Land Policy and Development* (Albuquerque, NM: University of New Mexico Press, 1996).

General Accounting Office Report RCED-04-241 (September 1994).

Goodrich, C. *Government Promotion of American Canals and Railroads, 1800–1890* (New York: Columbia University Press, 1960).

Graham, C. *The South Carolina State Constitution* (New York: Oxford University Press, 2011).

Greene, J. (ed.). *Colonial British America: Essays in the New History of the Early Modern Era* (Baltimore, MD: Johns Hopkins University Press, 1984).

Greene, J., R. Brana-Shute, and R. Sparks (eds). *Money, Trade and Power: The Evolution of Colonial South Carolina's Plantation Society* (Columbia: University of South Carolina Press, 2001).

Griffith, E. *History of American City Government: The Colonial Period* (New York: Oxford University Press, 1938).

___ *A History of American City Government: The Progressive Years and Their Aftermath, 1900–1920* (New York: Praeger, 1974).

Griswold, A. *Farming and Democracy* (New Haven, CT: Yale University Press, 1952).

Gunn, L. *The Decline of Authority* (Ithaca, NY: Cornell University Press, 1988).

Gunther, M. *The Wealthy 100: From Benjamin Franklin to Bill Gates—A Ranking of the Richest Americans, Past and Present* (Secaucus, NJ: Carol Pub. Group, 1996).

Hagstrom, J. "Born of the Dust Bowl," *Government Executive*, June 1, 1996.

___ "USDA Considers Consolidation," *Government Executive*, June 24, 1997.

Hagy, J. *This Happy Land: The Jews of Colonial and Antebellum Charleston* (Tuscaloosa, AL: University of Alabama Press, 1993).

Hammond, B. "Free Banks and Corporations: The New York Free Banking Act of 1838," 44 *Journal of Political Economy* 184 (1936).

Hanke, B. "Planned Unit Development and Land Use Intensity," 114 *University of Pennsylvania Law Review* 1 (1965).

___ (ed.). *The Homes Association Handbook* (Washington, DC: Urban Land Institute, 1966).

___ *et al. Planned Unit Development with a Homes Association*, FHA Land Planning Bulletin 6 (Washington, DC: HUD, 1963).

Hanke, B., and A. Faure. *Suggested Land Subdivision Regulations* (Washington, DC: Housing and Home Finance Agency, 1952).

Hanke, B., and R. Ekimoto. *Design Review: How Community Associations Maintain Peace and Harmony* (Arlington, VA: Community Associations Institute, reprinted 2004).

Hardin, C. *The Politics of Agriculture: Soil Conservation and the Struggle for Power in Rural America* (Glencoe, IL: Free Press, 1952).

Haskins, G. *Law and Authority in Early Massachusetts* (New York: Macmillan, 1960).

Hawke, D. *The Colonial Experience* (Indianapolis: Bobbs-Merrill, 1966).

Heath, M. "Public Railroad Construction and the Development of Private Enterprise in the South before 1861," 10 *Journal of Economic History*, Supplement (1950).

Hedges, J. *Building the Canadian West: The Land and Colonization Policies of the Canadian Pacific Railway* (New York: Macmillan, 1939).

Helms, D. "Hugh H. Bennett," in *American National Biography* (New York: Oxford University Press, 1999), vol. II.

___ "Hugh Hammond Bennett and the Creation of the Soil Erosion Service," 6 *Journal of Soil and Water Conservation* No. 2 (March–April 2009).

___ "Hugh Hammond Bennett and the Creation of the Soil Conservation Service, September 19, 1933–April 27, 1935," Natural Resources Conservation Service, Historical Insights No. 9 (March 20, 2010).

Hibbard, B. *A History of the Public Land Policies* (New York: Macmillan, 1924).

Hilkey, C. *Legal Development in Colonial Massachusetts, 1630–86* (New York: Columbia University Press, 1910).

Hofstadter, R. "William Leggett: Spokesman of Jacksonian Democracy," 58 *Political Science Quarterly* 581 (1943).

Honeywell, R. *The Educational Work of Thomas Jefferson* (Cambridge, MA: Harvard University Press, 1931).

Hsueh, V. "Giving Orders: Theory and Practice in the Fundamental Constitution of Carolina," 63 *Journal of the History of Ideas* 425 (2002).

Hurst, J. *Law and Social Order in the United States* (Ithaca, NY: Cornell University Press, 1977).

Hurst, W. *Law and the Conditions of Freedom in the Nineteenth Century United States* (Madison, WI: University of Wisconsin Press, 1956).

Hurt, R. *The Big Empty: The Great Plains in the Twentieth Century* (Tucson, AZ: University of Arizona Press, 2011).

Hyatt, W. "Common Interest Communities: Evolution and Reinvention," 31 *John Marshall Law School Law Review* 303, 379ff. (1998).

Ironstone, J. "Shaftesbury on Locke," 53 *American Political Science Review* (1959).

Jackson, K. *Crabgrass Frontier: The Suburbanization of the United States* (New York: Oxford University Press, 1985).

Janniskee, B. *Local Government in Early America* (Lanham, MD: Rowman & Littlefield, 2011).

Jennings, R. *The Creation of America: Through Revolution to Empire* (Cambridge: Cambridge University Press, 2000).

Johnson, P. "NRCS: Changing to Meet the Future," 94 *Journal of Forestry* 12 (1996).

Kenyon, D. "A New State VAT: Lessons from New Hampshire," 49 *National Tax Journal* 381 (1996).

Kirschten, E. *Catfish and Crystal* (Garden City, NY: Doubleday, 1960).

Klein, R. *Politics of the National Health Service* (London: Longmans, 2nd edn., 1989).

Koch, A., and W. Piden. *The Life and Selected Writings of Thomas Jefferson* (New York: Modern Library, 1944).

Lanza, M. *Agrarianism and Reconstruction Politics: The Southern Homestead Act* (Baton Rouge, LA: Louisiana State University Press, 1990).

Lautner, H. (ed.). *Subdivision Regulations: An Analysis of Land Subdivision Land Control Practices* (Chicago: Public Administration Service, 1941).

Levitan, S. *Swords into Plowshares: Our G.I. Bill* (Salt Lake City, UT: Olympus Pub. Co., 1973).

Levitt, R., and A. Wall, *The Reorganized National Health Service* (London: Croom Helm, 3rd edn., 1984).

Liebmann, G. "Suburban Zoning: Two Modest Proposals," 25 *Real Property, Probate and Trust Law Journal* 1 (1990).

___ "Land Readjustment for America: A Proposal for a Statute," 32 *Urban Lawyer* 1 (2000).

___ "The New American Local Government," 34 *Urban Lawyer* 93 (2002).

___ *Neighborhood Futures: Citizen Rights and Local Control* (New Brunswick, NJ: Transaction Books, 2003).

Lipscomb, A., and A. Bergh. *The Writings of Thomas Jefferson* (Washington, DC: Thomas Jefferson Memorial Assn., 1903).

Lively, R. "The American System: A Review Article," 29 *Business History Review* 81 (1966).

Loeb, I., and F. Shoemaker (eds). *Debates of the Missouri Constitutional Convention of 1875* (Columbia, MO: State Historical Society of Missouri, 1944).

Lowi, T. *The End of Liberalism* (New York: Norton, 2nd edn., 1977).

___ *The End of the Republican Era* (Norman, OK: University of Oklahoma Press, 1995).

McBain, H. *The Law and the Practice of Municipal Home Rule* (New York: Columbia University Press, 1916).

McGrane, R. *The Panic of 1837* (Chicago: University of Chicago Press, 1924).

McGuinness, C. "The Fundamental Constitutions of Carolina as a Tool for Lockean Scholarship," 17 *Interpretation* 127 (1989).

McKenzie, E. *Privatopia* (New Haven, CT: Yale University Press, 1994).

___ *Beyond Privatopia: Rethinking Residential Private Government* (Washington, DC: Urban Institute, 2011).

Maier, P. "The Revolutionary Origins of the American Corporation," 50 *William and Mary Quarterly* (3rd Series) 51 (1993).

Martin, J. *Profits in the Wilderness: Entrepreneurship and the Founding of New England Towns in the Seventeenth Century* (Chapel Hill, NC: University of North California Press, 1991).

Massachusetts Historical Society. *Winthrop Papers* (Boston: Massachusetts Historical Society, 1929).

Merrill, G. "John Wesley Powell," in *Dictionary of American Biography* (New York: Scribner, 1925), vol. VIII.

Messere, K. *Tax Policy in OECD Countries* (Amsterdam: BFD Publications, 1993).

Meyers, M. *The Jacksonian Persuasion: Politics and Belief* (Stanford, CA: Stanford University Press, 1957).

Middleton, R., and A. Lombard. *Colonial America: A History to 1763* (Oxford: Wiley-Blackwell, 4th edn., 2011).

Milton, J. "John Locke and the Fundamental Constitutions of Carolina," 21 *Locke Newsletter* 111 (1990).

Morgan, E. *The Puritan Dilemma: The Story of John Winthrop* (Boston: Little Brown, 1958).

Morgan, R. *Governing Soil Conservation: Thirty Years of the New Decentralization* (Baltimore, MD: Johns Hopkins University Press, 1965).

Morison, S. *Builders of the Bay Colony* (Oxford: Oxford University Press, 1930).

Morris, J. *Pulitzer: A Life in Politics, Print and Power* (New York: Harper, 2010).

Napier, T., S. Napier, and J. Tvrdon (eds). *Soil and Water Conservation Policies and Programs: Successes and Failures* (Boca Raton, FL: CRC Press, 2000).

National Association of Home Builders. *Home Builders' Manual for Land Development* (Washington, DC: NAHB, 1950).

National Resources Planning Board. *Public Works and Rural Land Use* (Washington, DC: GPO, 1942).

Nevins, A. *The State Universities and Democracy* (Urbana, IL: University of Illinois Press, 1962).

Oates, W. *The Political Economy of Fiscal Federalism* (Lexington, MA: Lexington Books, 1977).

Onuf, P. *Statehood and Union: A History of the Northwest Ordinance* (Bloomington, IN: Indiana University Press, 1987).

___ *Jefferson's Empire* (Charlottesville, VA: University Press of Virginia, 2000).

Parker, M. (ed.). *North Carolina Charters and Constitutions, 1578–1698* (Raleigh, NC: Carolina Charter Tercentenary Commission, 1963).

Parker, W. *The Life and Public Services of Justin Smith Morrill* (Boston: Houghton Mifflin, 1927).

Parrington, V. *The Colonial Mind, 1620–1800* (New York: Harcourt Brace, 1927).

Patton, C. *The Battle for Municipal Reform: Mobilization and Attack, 1875 to 1900* (College Park, MD: McGrath Pub. Co., 1969).

Peffer, E. *The Closing of the Public Domain: Disposal and Reservation Policies, 1900–1950* (Stanford, CA: Stanford University Press, 1951).

Peterson, M. *Thomas Jefferson and the New Nation* (New York: Oxford University Press, 1970).

___ (ed.). *Jefferson: Writings* (New York: Library of America, 1984).

Powell, J. *Report on the Lands of the Arid Region of the United States* (Cambridge, MA: Harvard University Press, 1962).

President's Research Committee on Social Trends. *Recent Social Trends* (New York: McGraw-Hill, 1933).

Primack, M. "Land Clearing under Nineteenth Century Techniques," 22 *Journal of Economic History* 484–97 (1962).

Procter, P. "William Leggett: Journalist and Literator," 44 *Papers of the Bibliographical Society of America* 239 (1950).

Pryce, A., and C. Bruere. *Timeshare Coming of Age* (London: Travel and Tourism Intelligence, 1999).

Rasmussen, S. "Neighborhood Planning," 27 *Town Planning Review* 197 (1957).

Rasmussen, W. *Taking the University to the People* (Ames, IA: Iowa State University Press, 1989).

Reed, T. *Municipal Government in the United States* (revised edn.) (New York: Appleton, 1934).

Reisner, M. *Cadillac West: The American West and Its Disappearing Water* (New York: Penguin, 1993).

Report of the Secretary of the Treasury on the Subject of Public Roads and Canals, 1808 (repr.) (New York: Augustus M. Kelley, 1968).

Richardson, J. (ed.). *Messages and Papers of the Presidents, 1789–1897* (Washington, DC: GPO, 1896).

Rivlin, A. *Reviving the American Dream* (Washington, DC: Brookings, 1992).

Rose, C. "The Comedy of the Commons," 53 *University of Chicago Law Review* 211, 781 (1986).

Ross, E. *Democracy's College: The Land Grant Movement in the Formative Stage* (New York: Arno, 1969).

Rutman, D. *Winthrop's Boston: Portrait of a Puritan Town* (Chapel Hill, NC: University of North California Press, 1965).

Sandalow, T. "The Limits of Municipal Power under Home Rule: A Role for the Courts," 48 *Minnesota Law Review* 643 (1964).

Sarson, S. *British America 1500–1800: Creating Colonies, Imagining an Empire* (London: Hodder, 2005).

Schlesinger, A. *The Age of Jackson* (Boston: Little, Brown, 1945).

Scott, R. *The Reluctant Farmer: The Rise of Agricultural Extension to 1949* (Urbana, IL: University of Illinois Press, 1971).

Sedgwick, T., Jr. (ed.). *A Collection of the Political Writings of William Leggett* (New York: Taylor and Dodd, 1840).

Seitz, D. *Joseph Pulitzer: Life and Letters* (London: Geoffrey Bles, 1926).

Seliger, M. *The Liberal Politics of John Locke* (London: Allen & Unwin, 1968).

Siegel, S. "The Public Role in Establishing Private Residential Communities," 38 *Urban Lawyer* 859 (2006).

Simeone, J. "Reassessing Jacksonian Political Culture: William Leggett's Egalitarianism," 4 *American Thought* No. 3 (2015).

Simms, D. *The Soil Conservation Service* (New York: Praeger, 1971).

Singer, P. "Bush and the Bureaucracy: A Crusade for Control," *Government Executive*, March 25, 2005.

Sirmans, E. *Colonial South Carolina: A Political History 1663–1763* (Chapel Hill, NC: University of North California Press, 1966).

Sklansky, J. *The Melodrama of Panic: William Leggett and the Literary Logic of Jacksonian Political Economy* (2007), at www.librarycompany.org/Economics/2007Conference/sklansky.pdf.

Sly, J. *Town Government in Massachusetts (1620–1930)* (Cambridge, MA: Harvard University Press, 1935).

Smith, P. *As a City upon a Hill: The Town in American History* (New York: Knopf, 1966).

Spann, E. *Ideals and Politics: New York Intellectuals and Liberal Democracy, 1820–1880* (Albany, NY: State University of New York Press, 1972).

Stabile, D. *Community Associations: The Emergence and Acceptance of a Quiet Innovation in Housing* (Westport, CT: Greenwood Press, 2000).

Stewart, F. *A Half Century of Municipal Reform: The History of the National Municipal League* (Berkeley, CA: University of California Press, 1950).

Stewart, M. "Cultivating Kudzu: The Soil Conservation Service and the Kudzu Distribution Program," 81 *Georgia Historical Quarterly* 151 (1997).

Strauss, R. "The EC Challenge to State and Local Governments," 16 *Intergovernmental Perspective* 13 (1990).

Stringfellow, K. *Jackrabbit Homestead: Tracing the Small Tract Act in the California Landscape, 1938–2008* (Chicago: University of Chicago Press, 2009).

Stuart, M. (ed.). *A Companion to Locke* (Oxford: Blackwell, 2016).

Symposium. "Home Owners' Associations as Private Governments," 21 *Public Administration Review* 535 (2011).

Taylor, A. *American Colonies: The Settling of North America* (New York: Penguin, 2001).

Teaford, J. *The Unheralded Triumph: City Government in America, 1870–1900* (Baltimore, MD: Johns Hopkins University Press, 1984).

Terrell, J. *The Man Who Rediscovered America: A Biography of John Wesley Powell* (New York: Weybright and Talley, 1969).

Trimble, W. "Diverging Tendencies in New York Democracy: The Period of the Loco-Focos," 24 *American Historical Review* 396 (1919).

___ "Social Philosophy of the Loco-Foco Democracy," 26 *American Journal of Sociology* 705, 711 (1921).

Turner, F. *The United States, 1830–1850* (New York: Holt, 1935).

Urban Land Institute. *Community Builders' Handbook* (Washington, DC: ULI, 1950).

Valandingham, K. "Constitutional Municipal Home Rule," 17 *William and Mary Law Review* 1 (1975).

Waldron, J. *God, Locke and Equality: Christian Foundations of John Locke's Political Thought* (Cambridge: Cambridge University Press, 2002).

Waterhouse, R. *A New World Gentry: The Making of a Merchant and Planter Class in South Carolina, 1670–1730* (New York: Garland, 1989).

White, L. *The Jeffersonians: A Study in Administrative History* (New York: Macmillan, 1951).

___ "William Leggett: Jacksonian Editorialist as Classical Liberal Political Economist," 18 *History of Political Economy* 307 (1986).

___ (ed.). *W. Leggett, Democratic Editorials: Essays in Jacksonian Political Economy* (Indianapolis: Liberty Press, 1984).

Whittier, J. *Old Portraits and Modern Sketches* (Boston: Ticknor and Fields, 1850).

___ *The Writings of John Greenleaf Whittier in Seven Volumes* (Cambridge, MA: Riverside, 1888).

Wiebe, R. *Self Rule: A Cultural History of American Democracy* (Chicago: University of Chicago Press, 1995).

Williams, R. *The Origins of Federal Support for Higher Education: George W. Atherton and the Land Grant College Movement* (University Park, PA: Penn State University Press, 1991).

Wilson, J. *Bryant and His Friends* (New York: Fords, Howard and Hulbert, 1886).

Wood, N. *John Locke and Agrarian Capitalism* (Berkeley, CA: University of California Press, 1984).

Woodbury, C. "Housing in the Development of American Cities," 25 *Land Economics* 397 (1949).

Wooton, D. (ed.). *John Locke: Political Writings* (Harmondsworth: Penguin, 1993).

Worster, D. *A River Running West: The Life of John Wesley Powell* (New York: Oxford, 2002).

Zuckerman, M. *Peaceable Kingdoms* (New York: Knopf, 1970).

INDEX